MW00477782

IFR Communications Manual

IFR Communications Manual

Radio Procedures for Instrument Flight

Bryan Harston

An Eleanor Friede Book
Macmillan Publishing Company • New York
Collier Macmillan Canada • Toronto
Maxwell Macmillan International
New York • Oxford • Singapore • Sydney

Macmillan Publishing Company
866 Third Avenue, New York, NY 10022

Collier Macmillan Canada, Inc.
1200 Eglinton Avenue East, Suite 200
Don Mills, Ontario M3C 3N1

Library of Congress Cataloging-in-Publication Data
Harston, Bryan.
    IFR communications manual : radio procedures for instrument flight/
by Bryan Harston.
        p.   cm.
"An Eleanor Friede book."
Includes index.
ISBN 0-02-548535-0
    1. Instrument flying.   2. Air traffic control.   I. Title.
TL711.B6H37   1990
629.132'5214—dc20   90-5557   CIP

This book is respectfully dedicated to the memory of two pilots with whom I never had the chance to fly: Howard E. Boggs and Colonel Richard D. Kimball, U.S.A.F. (Retired). Godspeed.

Contents

PART ONE
Learning to Speak IFR

PART TWO

Departure Communications

PART THREE

En Route Communications

PART FOUR

Arrival Communications

PART FIVE

Further Considerations

Acknowledgments

Writing this, my first book, was a lot like preparing for my first solo flight: It was at once terrifying and exhilarating, it took many more hours than I expected, and it is something I could never have accomplished alone.

Many thanks to everyone who helped with this book, especially the many pilots, controllers, and friends who have given freely of their time, advice, and experience. I owe a special debt of gratitude to Eleanor Friede; Steven Walker of Walker Creative, Inc.; Dean and Curtis Kimball; Steve Stephens; the controllers of the DAL TRACAB and the Dallas/Fort Worth TRACON; Pete Howard; and Robert Huff.

Carol and Bob, thanks for the genes, the environment, and the opportunities. Kelly, your support and guidance keep me going; I love you.

—BRYAN HARSTON

Dallas, Texas
January 1990

Introduction

Radio communication between pilots and air traffic controllers is part of practically every flight. Whether you fly through clouds all day or limit your travels to pattern flying in severely clear weather, the microphone is as much a tool of your craft as the yoke and rudder pedals. As our airspace fills up, everyone has to use the radio at some point during a flight. Even around private or uncontrolled fields, position reports are heard on an advisory frequency. On a clear day, the pilot on a VFR cross-country flight between two controlled airports may only use the radio twice—once at the departure airport, once at the destination—but the radio is still necessary for at least a little while.

When the weather goes down, however, things change. Radio communications become the *only* way to operate within the U.S. Airspace System. The radio is the pilot's link to the world outside the clouds. Without some way to tell ATC (Air Traffic Control) your position, receive instructions, copy clearances, and exchange weather information, safe instrument flight is impossible. It's not enough just to be able to talk on the radio. For IFR flight, you must be able to send and receive complete, accurate information. You must be able to *communicate* effectively with ATC.

Despite the increasing complexity of the ATC system, more and more pilots are acquiring instrument ratings without the benefit of communications training. The direct results of this trend are congested radio frequencies, misunderstood clearances, confused pilots, and frustrated controllers. The indirect result is a disorganized (read "dangerous") air traffic system.

As an instrument pilot, you trust your life to the integrity of the IFR system every day. Improving radio communications throughout the system will enhance its utility and widen the margin of safety within which we operate. This book is a vehicle for the instrument-rated pilot (or instrument student) to develop a better understanding of how IFR operations work and how communications bring the entire system together.

This is not an encyclopedia of different radio calls for every conceivable flight situation; it is more of an instructional text. The pilot learns to analyze the phases of an IFR flight and to communicate effectively under most circumstances.

Throughout this book, you'll see a fictitious aircraft number used, November 389KB. Any resemblance to an actual aircraft registration number is purely coincidental. When you read the sample radio calls herein, notice that all numbers except Zulu (Universal) times are spelled out (e.g. "Turn right to heading Zero–Six–Zero"). To avoid errors, numbers should always be pronounced one digit at a time over the radio. Similarly, airport and navaid identifiers are spelled out, using the phonetic alphabet (e.g., XYZ becomes X-Ray–Yankee–Zulu).

This book is the product of many minds and, as such, it is a composite of many diverse views. It was developed through the contributions of many air traffic controllers, flight instructors, and career pilots (private and professional, civilian and military). While it is based on the rules and conventions that govern the Air Traffic Control system, much of it includes matters of opinion. If you have a different system for managing IFR radio communications, and that system works, stick with it. This manual is for the rest of the pack, those pilots who know there is more to using the radio effectively than turning the fool thing on, but don't have a system of their own.

There is no single "right" way to use the radio during an instrument flight. There are, however, infinitely many "wrong" ways to get your point across to a controller. If you exert a little effort and eliminate just one bad radio habit from your regular operations, you'll be doing your part to clean up the airwaves and tighten up the slack in the IFR system. If that happens for you after you read this book, then perhaps I've done my part as well.

PART ONE

Learning to Speak IFR

CHAPTER 1

VFR vs. IFR Communications

What's the Difference?

To many VFR-only pilots, the instrument rating seems distant and enigmatic. What is it about the words "IN-STRUMENT AIRPLANE" on a pilot certificate that makes us instantly able to brave the elements and fly on cloudy days as well as clear? Why does the FAA (Federal Aviation Administration) require all those hours of dual instrument instruction? Why another stupid written exam? "After all," the VFR pilot mutters, "my instructor taught me to read flight instruments. I know how to keep the wings level by watching the attitude indicator. I use the DG (Directional Gyro) for heading changes, and I keep the ball in the center to coordinate my turns. So what's the trick? Why can't I fly through just that one layer of clouds to get home?"

How Tough Can It Be?

Most of these questions disappear the first time a VFR pilot flies in the right seat through hard IFR, watching and listening as a skilled instrument pilot slides the aircraft down the glide slope and breaks out of the murk lined up on the runway. When you observe it firsthand, the complexity of instrument flight is obvious. True, you can't know what mental gymnastics the pilot-in-command went through to steer the aircraft down safely, but you can sure hear every word on the radio, and it may seem puzzling:

"What? They cleared you to go *where*?"

"Maintain two thousand until established on what?"

"Contact the tower when?"

"What in the world is an 'intersection'?"

"How could you write all that down?"

And so it goes. Nothing the instrument-rated pilot does with the controls will be nearly as impressive or intimidating to a VFR pilot observer as the things said (and heard) on the radio during IFR flight.

None of this is to say that flying on instruments is easy—it's not. Yet, with enough effort and the right instruction, most pilots of average skill master the techniques of IFR operations. Sooner or later, your flight instructor will sign you off for your FAA check ride, and you'll perform the flight maneuvers just as you were taught. Suddenly, you wake up, and—boom!—you're instrument rated. You know how to maneuver the aircraft in instrument conditions. But *do you know how to fly within the system?* Where does an IFR flight start? Where and how do you file the flight plan? How do you "open" and "close" an IFR flight plan? What do you say? When? And to whom?

The Missing Link

This is the part that isn't easy—and normally isn't taught during instrument flight training: *Communicating and operating within the IFR system.* If you're like most pilots, you learned instrument flying under the hood, but in VFR conditions. On those flights, your instructor managed all the radio communications. Perhaps you even had to wait until your first dual IFR cross-country before the instructor let you tune the nav radios by yourself. The instructor's job was to teach you to fly on instruments, and that is what you learned. Federal Aviation Regulations, or FARs, don't require much specific training on radio procedures, and the instructor is busy enough just preparing you for the flight test.

The typical instrument check ride doesn't demand too much in the way of communications skills, either. True, the FAA requires "knowledge and use" of radio and clearance procedures, but you don't have to be "polished," or even "proficient" to pass the test. All examiners have you prepare an IFR flight plan as part of the check, but often the examinee won't file it with anyone. After the oral exam, you copy down a fictitious IFR "clearance" (spoken slowly and clearly) from the examiner. You take off and start to follow this "clearance," but then the examiner has you level off at a VFR altitude, and the rest of the check ride is maneuvers and approaches. No more cross-country flight plan. No actual practice at working with air traffic controllers. Many examiners even make the radio calls for you. Sure, there's nothing wrong with a helpful examiner at test time, but does a check ride like that really test your overall IFR skills?

Someday the new instrument pilot is going to fly within the ATC system, and the only way to operate within that system is to *communicate* with the people who make it work. The newly rated IFR pilot is much more familiar with how the airplane and instrument flying are supposed to work than with how the ATC system works. Of course, some VFR-only pilots operate in busy airspace and talk to controllers every day. But many more only use the radio once or twice on a cross-country flight. How do these pilots make the transition into the ATC system? Instrument flight training in the United States leaves many pilots to learn IFR communications the way the rest of us did—by trial and error.

Why isn't there more emphasis on communications in training and testing? Because it's not required by the rules. Why isn't it required by the rules? That's one of life's basic unanswerable questions. Ask any ten pilots how much communications training is enough, and you'll get ten different answers. But nearly all will agree on one thing— effective communication is critical for IFR flight.

The Need for Precise Communications

In true IFR weather conditions, air traffic controllers are the eyes of each aircraft in a given area. Controllers direct the three-dimensional flow of traffic via a tenuous radio voice link. The only way the controller can steer us—and the only way we can respond—is with the radio. The system works best when pilots and controllers talk to each other using standard phraseology, verifying everything.

This fragile radio link sometimes fails. Often, "communications failure" means a transmitter or receiver malfunction. But there is a more subtle type of failure. There are humans at each end of the radio conversation, and if either doesn't communicate effectively, the delicate ATC communications system fails just the same.

Misunderstood communications continue to cause many incidents and accidents, especially in busy traffic areas. A controller who misunderstands pilot intentions or reported altitude, or a pilot who accepts someone else's vector, takes the first step toward tragedy. In our increasingly controlled airspace system, it is imperative that pilots keep every transmission clear and concise, using standard phraseology whenever possible. This is especially important in busy terminal areas.

During the en route phase of an IFR flight, a misunderstood call sign, request, vector, or altitude may be fairly benign. At worst, it may lead to little more than a concerned voice on the radio. But during the departure or arrival phase of flight, especially in busy airspace, such a mistake can be fatal. In a crowded terminal area such as Dallas/Fort Worth's Regional Approach, you may be handed off three times within the last ten minutes of a flight in solid IFR. Trying to slow down, descend, and stabilize yourself on the approach while tuning to different frequencies and calling different controllers can be unnerving at best. You, as the pilot, must master the radio so that communicating is a reaction, not a distraction.

So What's the Big Deal About IFR Radio?

When I was a child, I spake as a child,
I understood as a child, I thought as a child. . . .
—I CORINTHIANS 13:11

Simply put, you're in the Big Leagues now. When you decide to join the ranks of IFR pilots flying within the ATC system, you put away the simpler trappings of VFR flight. It's no longer sufficient just to get cleared onto the active runway ("left turnout approved"), and then venture off into parts unknown. Now you have to tell someone where you are and where you're going at all times. You have to share frequencies with the pros. The controllers and the airline captains, the commuters and the corporate types, all talk to each other on the very same radio waves that you have to use. You'll hear the ARTCC (Air Route Traffic Control Center) clear some airliner to flight level 350, then in the same breath call some student in a Cessna 152 with a vector to heading 350° or with the latest altimeter setting.

What does this mean to you? First, *exposure*. When you're in cruise flight, controllers and other aircraft normally can't see what you're doing or how well you're doing it. Fly the clearance they give you, and ATC will never know what kind of pilot you are (or aren't). But VHF radio is like a party line in a small town: Everybody's listening, and what you say (and the way you say it) will affect others' perception of you.

Consider these two scenarios:

· You like to putter along at 70 knots in a ragged Tri-Pacer with your shirttail hanging out and your shoelaces untied, charts wadded up in the back and your hat stuck to your hair after you spilled a diet soda on it during the run-up. Yet each time you key the mike and call Center, you sound like the commander of the Space Shuttle.

Or:

· You are Captain Precision in a spit-shined King Air, without so much as a hair or pencil out of place, flying within 4 feet of your assigned altitude and calculating fuel burn to the nearest teaspoon. But when you call Approach Control, you stammer like a nervous teenager.

Which pilot sounds like a professional? Which will Center take more seriously? Who moves more smoothly within the IFR system? Right—the Space Shuttle commander. Why? Human nature. The only way a controller or another pilot can assess your skills is by listening to you.

The second thing IFR communication means to you is *safety*. As explained above, the IFR system is a complex machine that depends upon every part (pilots and controllers) functioning properly. If pilots resort to nonstandard terminology or respond to detailed clearances with a simple "Roger," then the machine breaks down and safety may be compromised.

The last, and least obvious, benefit of skilled IFR communication is *simplicity*. The more proficient you become at communicating with others during IFR flight, the more precise and relaxed each flight becomes. As you gain experience, you're able to predict what your next assigned frequency will be and who you'll be calling. You can anticipate what they'll tell you to do when you call. As a direct result, your inflight workload becomes easier to manage, and the IFR flight forms itself into logical segments.

The ideal flight is a flight without surprises—and that means planning and skill in every area, including communications. Skill in using the airwaves is a valuable tool for making life at the controls simpler. The purpose of this book is to help pilots develop some of these skills.

CHAPTER 2

First Things First

Tips for Better Inflight Communications

Many factors influence the way we sound on the radio and the way the radio sounds to us. There are two basic qualities to your "sound" on the radio: (1) the quality of the radio signal transmitted; and (2) the words you choose to express your message. You may have the finest microphone available, a world-class speaking voice, and a static-free transmitter, but if you "er . . . ah . . . um" your way through each transmission you'll still sound like a rank amateur to everyone else on the frequency. On the other hand, you can achieve a clear, professional sound with minimal equipment if you just take the time to choose your words carefully and speak clearly.

Sounding Your Best, Part I: Better Signals

So what affects the quality of the signal transmitted? Some factors are obvious, like cabin background noise, speaker size, and quality of the microphone or transmitter. Others are more subtle. Microphone position, the volume of your voice, and even the way you press the push-to-talk button can improve or impair the signal you broadcast.

Some things are beyond the pilot's control, at least in flight. Radio frequency interference, or RFI, is a type of noise that usually results from stray emissions by alternators, generators, magnetos, electric motors, or even unshielded wiring. RFI can produce an annoying whine, popping, or crackling in your radio signal. Sometimes just the position of power cables or antenna leads, or frayed insulation on a spark plug wire, will so degrade a broadcast signal that listeners hear only noise and broken syllables. If you own an aircraft, a good avionics shop can help you locate and eliminate most sources of RFI in your radios. Renters are stuck with the radio installation available in the planes they fly.

No matter how good or bad your avionics, you can be a better communicator simply by using radio equipment properly. The factors you *can* control are covered in more detail below.

Sounding Your Best, Part II: Better Words

All other factors being equal, the pilot who carefully chooses words and who thinks through every transmission before calling is the better communicator. Sure, there is standard terminology you should use on the radio, and there are common terms you should *avoid* when possible. But it's not necessary to memorize the *Airman's Information Manual* to become a good IFR communicator. Even if you deviate from ATC's rigid phraseology when speaking, you can make all your radio calls short, clear, accurate, and complete if you ask yourself these three questions before you key the mike:

1. Whom am I talking to? To know the answer to this question, you must first know where you are *geographically*. That's part of your instrument navigation skills and isn't taught in this manual. In addition, knowing the answer requires understanding *where you are in the flight*. This means learning the phases of IFR flight, and learning whom you talk to during each phase. In most cases you'll be calling (*a*) a local facility (tower or ground control); (*b*) a regional facility (the TRA-CON, or Terminal Radar Approach CONtrol); or (*c*) an en route facility (the ARTCC, or Center).

2. Why am I calling them? Once you understand what the phases of IFR flight are, and what phase you're in at any particular moment, you'll know why you're calling someone. It doesn't matter whether you are handed off between controllers or if you have a request or a report to make. If you first think about whom it is you're contacting, you'll know why you're contacting them.

3. What will they want to know when I call? The answer to this is a function of question 2—*why* you're calling determines *what* you say. It's perhaps the most difficult of the three questions to answer, but one you can master with this book and a little practice.

   Sometimes ATC merely wants to know that you've switched frequencies after a handoff. Other times, they'll want to know who you are, where you are, your altitude, and your ETA at your next reporting point. If your initial radio contact gives ATC all the information they need in a clear, brief transmission, you save the controller and other pilots the aggravation of tying up a frequency with needless question-and-answer exchanges.

When you know the answers to these three questions before you ever pick up a microphone, you've mastered the essence of effective, professional IFR communications. In the following chapters, these questions are addressed for every phase of IFR flight.

So How Long Until I've Learned All This?

It's not necessary to read every radio call from a script. It would be better to review the principles contained herein and then choose phrases you're comfortable with. When you first learned to fly, you reached a point where your skills lost the stiff, mechanical feel of the trainee and became smooth, precise actions. The same will happen with your radio skills. After you communicate in the ATC system for a time, you'll pick up certain phrases and "magic words" you like to use when contacting ATC. In time, the jargon of IFR flight becomes second nature to you and you become a confident user of the IFR system.

The rest of this chapter is devoted to some basic rules for using the comm radios and other equipment in any flight environment, VFR or IFR. These principles help others understand you more easily and thus reduce the likelihood of a misunderstanding with ATC.

Headsets and Intercoms: There Oughta Be a Law.

It's amazing that there are still flight instructors out there who permit their students to fly without a headset. The headset is arguably the most overlooked and underused piece of safety equipment available to pilots today. Some say they should be mandatory equipment for instrument training. Common sense suggests likewise.

A "headset" is not to be confused with "headphones." The former is just what the name implies—it is one or two earphones mounted together, in a *set*, with a boom microphone. As a unit, the headset provides the pilot with cleaner, clearer sound from the radios, along with a microphone that's always in place and never occupies the hands during a busy approach.

Noise-attenuating headsets are ideal for the deafening environment of the small piston-powered aircraft cockpit. Without headsets, such a cockpit is a rattling, blaring box of wind roar and engine noise. In order to hear the radio, occupants turn up the volume loud enough to hear the speaker over the din. This increases the overall noise level in the cockpit, and can make the radio unintelligible by distorting the sound coming out of the speaker. These factors combine to increase the risk of mistakes in communications between pilot and controller, and can cause permanent hearing loss after a few years.

As if garbled reception and hearing loss aren't enough, recent research indicates that exposure to cockpit noise, even on shorter flights, induces pilot fatigue. Fatigue in any amount is a pilot's enemy. It degrades pilot performance in subtle ways, slowing reflexes or leading to errors in judgment.

A noise-attenuating headset eliminates these problems. Soundproofed earpieces eliminate most of the background roar in the cockpit, shielding the speakers and the pilot's ears from the outside clamor. This not only decreases the strain on the pilot's ears, but also permits a lower volume setting for the radio, further reducing the overall noise level for the pilot. Besides saving the pilot's hearing over the long haul, reduced noise means less pilot fatigue and better comprehension of controllers' instructions.

Having a microphone permanently poised at your lips

may sound intimidating, but to the single pilot it's a god-send. The first time you try to fly a stabilized approach to minimums alone, in turbulence, you'll come to despise hand-held microphones. There are power controls, flaps, gear, and radios to work with your right hand. Your left hand is busy flying the airplane. So which hand is free to grab the microphone and talk to ATC when the ride gets rough? A headset microphone is always in place, and allows you to transmit simply by pushing a button on the control yoke with one finger. What's more, you don't have to hold your head still when you talk. The headset follows your head around as you scan for traffic in clear air, thereby enhancing safety even more.

One often-overlooked benefit of using a headset is the "sidetone." This is a feature of most modern radios which, like a telephone, allows you to hear your own voice when you transmit. The sidetone allows you to hear how you sound, which helps you develop a better speaking style on the radio.

In the teaching or co-piloting environment, an intercom with headsets is the only way to manage communications. A voice-activated intercom allows pilot and instructor to speak in normal tones without shouting over the noise of the aircraft. Incoming and outgoing radio calls are heard through the same headset as the intercom, and most intercoms give priority to incoming radio signals, so conversation between crew members doesn't obscure ATC's calls. An intercom allows the cockpit to be just as relaxing and productive a teaching environment as the classroom.

One additional reason headsets are so important for the student pilot: Most students don't understand *any* aircraft radio calls at first. Even when listening to a scanner while sitting in the relative calm of the instructor's office, the typical student can hear and understand the words, but won't begin to comprehend their *meaning*. When that student then moves to the noisy cockpit of a single-engine trainer, it becomes a challenge for our budding pilot to hear the radio speaker *at all,* much less to understand and respond to what is said. Put a noise-attenuating headset on the student, and suddenly radio calls become audible and understandable. Every step we can take to make life in the cockpit a little easier on the student pilot enhances safety and makes the learning process a little less traumatic.

If you fly light aircraft and don't have a noise-attenuating headset, get one. Your ears, your nerves, and ATC will thank you for it. By reducing the risk of hearing loss, you may avoid future troubles in keeping your FAA medical certificate. If you're a pilot in training, insist that your instructor use a headset and intercom with you. If necessary, buy a portable intercom and extra headset yourself. For the cost of a few hours' instrument dual time, you can buy a decent intercom and headset from most pilot shops or mail-order houses. The investment will pay for itself now and for the rest of your flying years.

Microphone Use (Just Like the Telephone, Only Different)

The closest many people ever come to using a microphone is singing with a hairbrush in front of the bathroom mirror. Assuming you don't have a bathroom mirror in the cockpit, the microphone will have to do. If you find yourself using a hand-held microphone instead of a headset (tsk, tsk—didn't you read the last section?), you can still optimize its performance by using it properly. First, hold the microphone very close to your mouth when speaking. Most aircraft microphones are of the noise-canceling variety. This means they screen out unwanted background noise, making your voice easier to understand over the radio. In order for this feature to work properly, however, you must speak directly into the microphone. If you hold it too far away from your mouth, the microphone will pick up the cockpit noise as the primary signal, and screen out your voice as background noise.

How close is close enough? Most headset manufacturers recommend adjusting boom microphones to actually brush against your lips when talking. Hand-held microphones should be held directly in front, or at the corner, of your mouth, no more than one inch away from your lips.

Whether you use a headset or hand-held microphone, you will have a push-to-talk switch to deal with. With headsets or intercoms, you have a switch somewhere on or near the control yoke. On hand-helds, the switch is on the microphone itself. Regardless of where the switch is, the procedure is the same:

- Press the switch firmly *before* you start to talk. Don't cut off your first words—e.g., "(click) is with you at three thousand." Be sure you press the button all the way in and hold it like that throughout your transmission. A broadcast from a half-on, half-off microphone is impossible to understand, so be sure it's firmly on.
- Don't release the switch until *after* you're finished. It's frustrating for a controller to hear most, but not all, of every radio call a pilot makes: "Center, Two–Three–X-ray is with you, level at (click)."

Proper use of radio hardware starts with the parts you speak into and listen to—microphones and speakers. But of equal importance is the way you use the electronics themselves—the radio transmitter/receiver.

Tuning, Volume, and Squelch

You don't have to be an engineer to understand your radio, although it helps. You don't even have to know what a radio wave looks like, much less how a radio sends or receives them, to use one properly. Still, you should know the latitude, longitude, and function of every knob, switch, button, and lever in any airplane you fly.

The best way to learn about your radio is to read the manufacturer's instructions. If no written instructions are available, you should have an instructor or radio technician explain the features of your radio stack. However, here are a few guidelines to help you adjust aircraft radios, regardless of make or model, for optimum listening quality.

The first thing to do is turn the radio on. Obvious as this seems, almost everyone has, at one time or another, called and called frantically with no response—and then discovered the radio was turned off, or down, or the microphone wasn't plugged in. Locate the power switch on your radio and turn it off, then on. Be sure you feel the switch lock positively into position. Don't rely on the position of the volume knob to show you it's on; those knobs sometimes pull off and are replaced incorrectly. If you have a power light, or a digital display, you'll know when the power is on. Otherwise, unless the frequency is active, you have to adjust the squelch to know for sure (see below).

The next thing to do is properly tune your radio. Again, if you have an electronically tuned radio, it's easy. If you have rotary tuning knobs or plastic digits showing through small windows, you have to be sure the tuner "clicks" positively into place when tuning. After tuning in a new frequency, always allow the radio a few seconds to tune in before you transmit. Just because you've switched the dial doesn't mean the tuner has locked in yet. Besides, waiting a second or two allows you to *listen* first to see if the frequency is busy. It's irritating when someone switches to a new frequency and immediately keys the microphone to talk while someone else is already transmitting. Then neither call will be heard by anyone, and whoever was talking before will have to repeat the message.

One other hint about listening: ATC often handles military aircraft on the same frequencies you use. The military transmit on ultra-high-frequency (UHF) sets, however, so you don't hear their calls; you just hear ATC's side of the conversation. Never assume, therefore, that a controller is ignoring you if you hear ATC talking but can't get a response to your call. The sector may be filled with military traffic.

When you first set up your radios for a flight, you also need to adjust the volume and squelch controls for the best sound. In oversimplified terms, the squelch is basically a static barrier with a sensitivity control on it. By adjusting the sensitivity, you decide how much background static is filtered out. Set the sensitivity to its highest level (the squelch turned all the way down), and you'll hear every radio broadcast in range, complete with roaring static and noise on the frequency when no one is transmitting. Set the sensitivity at the lowest setting (the squelch turned all the way up), and you'll get pleasant silence. Even when the tower calls—silence; you won't hear any radio traffic at all. The squelch is filtering out everything.

Proper squelch and volume settings are easy to make. The following steps work with nearly every type of comm radio:

- Turn the volume all the way down. This is to protect your ears against a burst of noise from an unknown volume setting.

- Turn the squelch all the way down (to the highest sensitivity level). The radio will now receive continuous static, as well as all calls within the area.

- Slowly increase the volume until the static (or radio traffic) is at a comfortable listening level.

- Turn the squelch up slowly. At some point, the background static between calls will stop, and the silence will be broken only by transmissions from other radios. Increase the squelch just slightly higher than this level, and stop. This will give you the squelch setting you want. It keeps out static while it allows strong radio signals to break through and be heard.

A last hint about volume settings: Check to be sure the volume control on your headset (if you have one) is set fairly high before adjusting the radio volume. If the headset is turned down too low, the natural tendency is to turn the radio up much higher. This forces the radio's amplifier to work harder than it would if it were turned down and the headset volume turned up. If the radio volume is too high, with the headset volume adjusted too low, the result is distorted, scratchy sound. Of course, minor adjustments of either control should not affect sound quality too greatly, but you should avoid extremes.

The last, and possibly most important, area of radio equipment management is knowing how to avoid a "stuck mike." A sticky push-to-talk button, a Jepp binder laid atop a microphone, or a loose microphone jack may cause your comm radio to stick in the "transmit" mode. If you're transmitting without realizing it, you can't receive any further information from ATC, some of which may be crucial to the safety of your flight. What's more, you effectively jam all communications on that frequency, depriving all aircraft on that channel of any means of talking to ATC.

There could be as many as fifteen or twenty aircraft assigned to that frequency, all depending upon its being available. A stuck microphone is an emergency situation, so don't be the culprit. If your radio has a TX or Xmit symbol that lights when you key the microphone, be sure it doesn't stay lit when you release the button. Make sure, if all the radio traffic suddenly goes silent, it's not because you're monopolizing the entire frequency.

Write It Down!

When you first learned VFR cross-country navigation, your instructor taught you to have your flight plan all written up before you left. You had a pad and pencil handy, and you checked off times and mileages carefully all along the way. No detail escaped notation on your knee board.

This is a habit that every IFR pilot should develop. Always have a pen or pencil within your reach, and have at least a small blank note pad available. Clearances, frequencies, and altitudes come at you from several directions at various times during every flight. By developing the habit of writing everything down when ATC calls, you increase your accuracy and thus your safety.

Figures 2.1 through 2.5 illustrate one way to fit all necessary communications information onto one sheet of paper on your lap. A written record like this allows you to recheck your clearance at any time, and helps you remember what altitude you were told to descend to. What's more, it gives you a running list of the frequencies you've been assigned during the flight. This is useful for those occasions when you get no response on a *new* assigned frequency. You can retune the old frequency and tell Center that you can't make contact on the new one. Without the old frequency in front of you, you have to consult the en route charts or some other source to know whom to call for help. This is rarely a life-threatening situation, but it's annoying and unnecessary. Keeping a clear record of clearances, altitudes, and frequencies throughout the flight is yet another tactic that the professional uses to stay organized and think ahead.

Using any blank note pad (I recommend the 5-by-7-inch size), create a blank communications log form, as shown in Figure 2.1. Figures 2.2 through 2.5 show how information accumulates on the log during the flight, until at last you land with a complete record, including all frequencies, amended clearances, and ATIS (Automatic Terminal Information Service) information from the departure and destination airports.

Your Readback Is Correct

Always repeat instructions back to a controller. It's fine to abbreviate the readback, but be sure you give ATC enough of a response so that they can correct you if you got it wrong. For example, suppose you're level at 6,000 feet and ATC calls you: "Cessna One–One–Alpha, descend and maintain three thousand." It's not enough to answer, "One–One–Alpha, Roger," since ATC won't know if you're copying the new altitude, starting down now (as you should) or later, or even if you have the new altitude right. What's more, the FAA requires pilots to report leaving any assigned altitude. For these reasons, a better response is, "One–One–Alpha leaving six thousand for three thousand."

To avoid confusion and prevent mistakes in communications, it's safest to read back all items which involve instructions, clearances, or other vital data. How do you

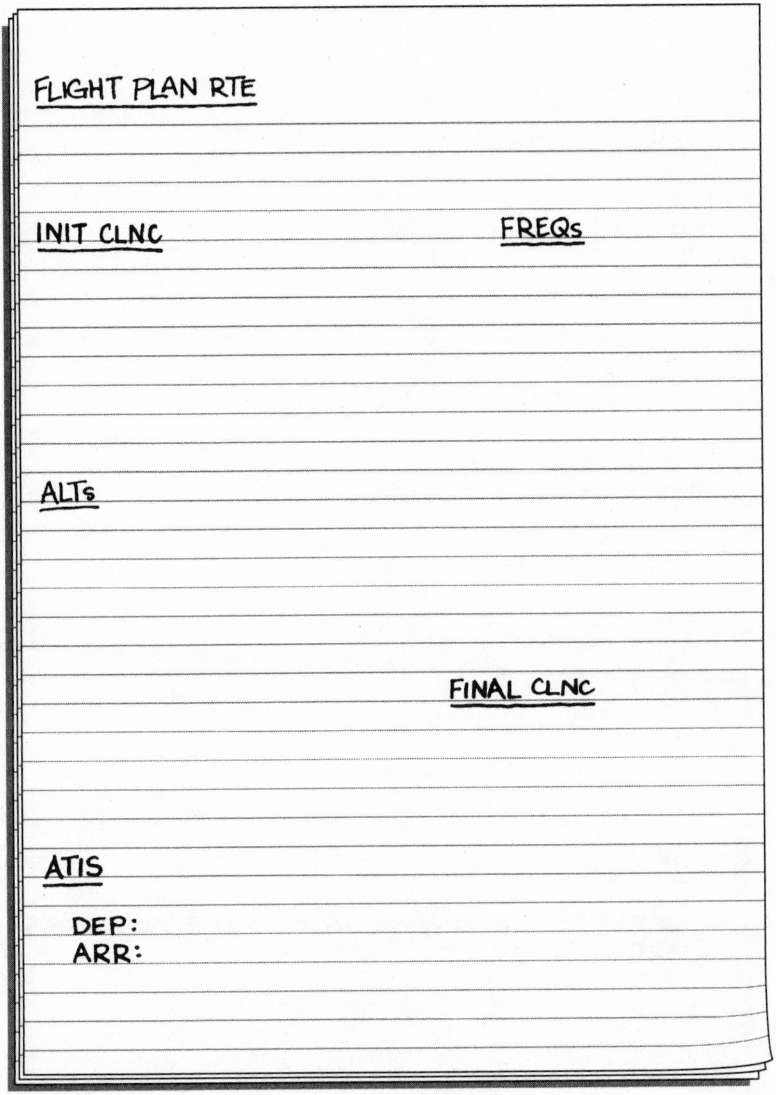

Figure 2.1
IFR communications log using 5 by 7 notepad.

FLIGHT PLAN RTE

ADS ⟶ ADM v358 OKC

INIT CLNC   FREQs

ALTs

FINAL CLNC

ATIS

DEP: ☒ 0150ꝫ/CLR v15 62/55 350/5 30.11 RY33
ARR:

Figure 2.2

Copy your flight-planned route onto the log. If your clearance is
"As Filed," you'll have the route in front of you. After you get
the current ATIS information, you're ready to call for your
clearance.

FLIGHT PLAN RTE

ADS ⊅• ADM v358 OKC

INIT CLNC	FREQs
C OKC APT V: p̄ DEP	124.3
RY HDG 500', Ⓣ️Ⓡ 020°	
RV CELIN △, CAF.	
M20, XP 80 p̄ 10.	
124.3 2667	

ALTs

20

FINAL CLNC

ATIS

DEP: ☒ 0150z/CLR VIS 62/55 350/5 30.11 RY33
ARR:

Figure 2.3

After copying the clearance, copy your initial altitude assignment and departure frequency into the "ALTs" and "FREQs" columns. The symbols and abbreviations shown in these figures are discussed in chapter 6.

FLIGHT PLAN RTE

ADS D→ ADM v358 OKC

INIT CLNC   FREQs

C OKC APT v: p̄ DEP   ~~124.3~~
RY HDG 500', ⓉⓇ 020°   ~~118.1~~
RV CELIN △, CAF.   125.35
M20, XP 80 p̄ 10.
124.3 2667

ALTs

~~20~~
~~160~~
↑M80

                                    FINAL CLNC

ATIS

DEP: ☒ 0150z/CLR v15 62/55 350/5 30.11 RY33
ARR:

Figure 2.4

As the flight continues, copy each new altitude or frequency
assignment in the appropriate column, then draw a single line
through the previous assignment.

FLIGHT PLAN RTE

ADS Đ→ ADM v358 OKC

INIT CLNC   FREQs

C OKC APT V: p̄ DEP   124.3
RY HDG 500', (TR) 020°   118.1
RV CELIN △, CAF.   125.35
M20, XP 80 p̄ 10.   118.5
124.3 2667   121.7

ALTs

20
↑60
↑M80
↓50
↓30
                              FINAL CLNC

                              (TR) 350° M25 TIL
                              EST LOC, C ILS
                              RY 35R
                              TWR @ MKR
ATIS

DEP: ☒ 0150z/CLR V15 62/55 350/5 30.11 RY33
ARR: Ⓗ 0230z 20 OVC, 150 BKN V3 57/54
        330/11 G 17 29.97 ILS 35R

Figure 2.5

As you near the destination, listen to the ATIS and copy your
final approach clearance.

decide whether a readback is needed? Just ask yourself, "Could this information endanger the flight if I misunderstood it?" Under this analysis, you should *always* repeat frequencies, vectors, amended clearances, taxi instructions, or any runway clearance (position and hold, cleared for takeoff, cleared to land). It's usually *not* necessary to repeat altimeter settings (unless the new setting is grossly different from the prior setting), weather updates, or other calls that are merely advisory in nature.

Identify Your Audience—and Yourself

In radio communications, as in any situation, two people sometimes converse with each other about two entirely different things, each believing the other means something else. In fact, a pilot and controller might discuss a clearance at length before one or the other realizes the clearance is meant for someone else. In order to avoid confusion as to who is supposed to respond to your radio call, *always* state the name of the facility you are talking to at the beginning of any radio call. This serves two purposes: (1) it alerts a controller if you're on the wrong frequency (e.g., calling for Kansas City Center on a frequency used by ground control at Wichita should result in your error being pointed out to you); and (2) it advises a facility what service you require (e.g., calling a TRACON "departure" tells them you've just taken off, calling them "approach" tells them you're inbound to the area).

For the same reasons, you should always recite your aircraft ID number when calling *or responding* to a controller. The first time you speak to that controller, give your entire aircraft tail number. For all subsequent responses, you can abbreviate the number to the last three numbers or letters. For example, if you are handed off from Atlanta

Center to Memphis Center, your first radio call would be:

MEMPHIS CENTER, TWIN CESSNA THREE–
EIGHT–NINER–KILO–BRAVO WITH YOU,
LEVEL AT ONE–SIX THOUSAND.

Memphis Center might respond:

NOVEMBER THREE–EIGHT–NINER–KILO–
BRAVO, RADAR CONTACT. NASHVILLE ALTIM-
ETER TWO–NINER–NINER–SEVEN.

It normally isn't necessary to read back altimeter settings, but you should still acknowledge Memphis' call. You
may simply reply: NINER–KILO–BRAVO, ROGER. For
this call, and all other calls to this controller, you may refer
to yourself as "Niner–Kilo–Bravo."* Always use some form
of your aircraft number when talking to ATC. Otherwise,
neither the controller nor other aircraft know who is talking.

In Conclusion: It's Your Voice

Inflight communications depend on a great many factors,
in both hardware and personnel. Proper use of the two-
way radio enhances safety and comfort levels whether you
are a pilot or controller. But in order to make the VHF

---

* Be careful, however, about using an "abbreviated" call sign in a
busy area. Occasionally two different aircraft have call signs ending with
the same three letters or numbers. For example, if you are flying Twin
Cessna 3–8–9–K–B and another pilot is nearby in Cherokee 1–1–9–
K–B, both call signs would become "Niner–Kilo–Bravo" when shortened by you or a controller. In such a situation, you *must* use your entire
call sign (especially the aircraft type—in this instance, Cessna) to prevent confusion and possible disaster. Using shortened call signs is generally acceptable and reduces frequency congestion, but only vigilance
and concentration will consistently keep you out of trouble.

frequencies more livable for all of us, one last factor comes into play—tone of voice. Consider a simple transmission by a controller:

TWIN CESSNA THREE–EIGHT–NINER–KILO–
BRAVO, DESCEND AND MAINTAIN SEVEN
THOUSAND.

And consider your reply:

NINER–KILO–BRAVO, ROGER, OUT OF EIGHT
THOUSAND FOR SEVEN THOUSAND.

Read the above transmissions to yourself twice: once in a friendly, accommodating tone, and once in an abrupt, order-giving manner. Makes quite a difference, doesn't it? As in any aspect of life, the way we treat others determines how they treat us. Since you will be in constant contact with various controllers throughout every IFR flight, you may as well make the effort to be pleasant to them. You will almost certainly receive the same consideration in return.

The quality of radio traffic in the skies depends upon all of us working together to standardize and streamline communications. With a little work and a little practice, every pilot can learn to communicate well and interact smoothly with the ATC system on every flight.

CHAPTER 3

A Few Choice Words

The Lexicon of Air Traffic Control

Before you master the craft of IFR communications, you need to know what controllers are saying when they call. The first and best way to learn what words to expect when flying IFR, and what those words mean, is to *listen*. Expose yourself to active ATC frequencies whenever possible. If you have a portable comm radio or a scanner, you can monitor a local tower or approach facility; otherwise, tune your aircraft radio to an en route Center frequency, even when you're just flying around VFR. Better yet, ask for VFR flight following the next time you're going cross-country. If the controller has time, you will be given a discrete transponder code and handled in much the same way as IFR traffic (at least in terms of radio communications). Listening to controllers and IFR traffic gives valuable experience to the novice communicator.

Another ideal source of communications know-how is the *Airman's Information Manual,* or *AIM.* The *AIM* is one of those items every pilot should have—and use. It's published every 112 days by the FAA, and annually by several private publishers. It's usually sold in combination with the FARs. The *AIM* is voluminous and hardly qualifies as entertaining reading; but if you set aside the time to read a few sections a day over a period of weeks, you'll gain a wealth of useful and potentially life-saving knowledge.

The portions of the *AIM* we're concerned with here are chapter 4, section 2 ("Radio Communications Phraseology and Techniques") and section 4 ("ATC Clearance/ Separations"), along with the "Pilot/Controller Glossary" following chapter 8. Together they are the bible for communicating with ATC, and the source of the standard terminology used by controllers and professional pilots. The *AIM* defines nearly every term you're ever likely to hear on the radio (and many you never will). Its lessons are beyond the scope of this work. Still, there are a few basic terms and phrases from the *AIM* that make up the core of a solid IFR communications vocabulary. They carry particular meanings which serve as shorthand for communicating specific information to others. The glossary in this chapter lists only a few of these terms and phrases, along with tips on how to use them.

The study of ATC phraseology serves a dual purpose. It helps you formulate clearer, more succinct radio calls, and it makes it easier to understand what ATC is saying *to you*. Not every pilot sticks to precise phraseology all the time (in fact, it's doubtful that *any* pilot does). Controllers, on the other hand, communicate "by the book" nearly all the time. If you learn their language, you can better understand and respond to them.

The purpose of this chapter isn't to teach you what words *not* to use on the radio. There is one common radio term, however, which is so misunderstood that it deserves special treatment. The term is "Roger." It is a term of acknowledgment, and means that you have received a transmission. It is *only* an acknowledgment. *"Roger" does not mean "Yes,"* nor does it mean "Okay, I'll do what you say," nor even "I understood everything you said." Probably the most misused term among American pilots, "Roger" is a real potential trouble source for anyone who uses it.

The problem seems to be this: Everyone has heard "Roger" used as standard radio babble in movies, on TV, and at airports all around the country. It was originally a military term, and almost two generations grew up using it or hearing it at some point in their lives. Naturally, if we hear something often enough, we may resort to using it ourselves. Unfortunately, since "Roger" means different things to different people, it is likely to cause confusion among those on the air. There are two common situations in which you'll hear this term misused:

- *Used to mean "affirmative"*: Center asks, "Cessna Five–Five–Delta, are you receiving the Scurry VOR?" "Roger," you reply. This doesn't really answer the question; it merely acknowledges that you heard it. The proper response to this question is "Affirmative" or "Negative."

- *Used instead of reading back instructions*: This is the most dangerous use of "Roger." If you're assigned a new altitude, given an amended clearance, or cleared to cross an active runway, the safety of your aircraft and all those around you rely on some form of readback. When a controller only hears "Roger," it's impossible to know who spoke, much less what the speaker is acknowledging.

Since your goal (as an effective radio communicator) is to be clearly understood by all who hear you, your choice of words is important. If you avoid using ambiguous, confusing, or incorrect terms in your radio use, you decrease the likelihood of a communications breakdown between you and ATC.

BRIEF GLOSSARY OF ATC TERMINOLOGY

Most of the following words, phrases, and definitions come from the *AIM*'s "Pilot/Controller Glossary." While some of the most-used terms are included, this is hardly an exhaustive listing, since the Glossary includes over four hundred terms and phrases. For a complete list of FAA/ATC terminology as well as that of the ICAO (International Civil Aviation Organization), refer to the complete *Airman's Information Manual.*

Advise intentions: "Tell me what you plan to do." This is normally used by ATC when a pilot declares a missed approach or faces some change in a planned flight.

Affirmative: "Yes." This and "Negative" are the only proper responses to a yes–or–no question.

Air Route Traffic Control Center (ARTCC): Usually referred to as "Center," this facility provides air traffic control service to aircraft operating on IFR flight plans within controlled airspace (primarily during the en route phase of flight). An ARTCC may also provide limited flight following services to VFR traffic when equipment capability and controller workloads permit.

Clearance void if not off by (time): When used by ATC as part of a clearance, this phrase advises a pilot that the clearance will be canceled if the aircraft does not take off by a specified time. If the void time expires, the pilot must obtain a new clearance or cancel the IFR flight plan prior to departure.

Cleared as filed: The aircraft is cleared to proceed in

accordance with the route of flight filed in the flight plan. This clearance will not include the altitude, SID (Standard Instrument Departure), or SID Transition.

Cleared for (type of) *approach*: The aircraft is cleared to execute a specific instrument approach procedure to an airport; e.g., "Cleared for ILS Runway Three–One Left approach."

Cleared for the option: ATC authorizes the aircraft to make a touch-and-go, low approach, missed approach, stop-and-go, or full-stop landing at the discretion of the pilot. This clearance is normally used in training so that an instructor can evaluate a student's performance under changing situations.

Cross (fix) *at* (altitude): This is an altitude restriction. ATC directs the aircraft to cross the named fix at a specific altitude. If the aircraft cannot climb or descend to that altitude safely before reaching the fix, the pilot must advise the controller.

Sometimes the altitude is stated as "at or above" or "at or below" a certain altitude. In that case, the aircraft may cross the named fix above (or below) the named altitude, but may not climb or descend beyond an earlier altitude limit.

Direct: Straight-line flight between two navigational aids, fixes, points, or any combination thereof. When "direct" is used by pilots to describe off-airway routes, the points that define direct-route segments become compulsory reporting points (unless the aircraft is in radar contact).

Flight level: A level of constant atmospheric pressure related to the reference datum of 29.92 inches of mercury. Each flight level is stated in three digits that represent hundreds of feet. For example, "flight level 230" represents a barometric altimeter indication of 23,000 feet; "flight level 195" represents 19,500 feet. In ATC terminology, flight levels are used for altitudes of 18,000 feet ("flight level 180") and higher.

Go ahead: "Proceed with your message." This term is never used as authorization to "go ahead" with anything except transmitting a message. For example, you should never be told "go ahead" if you ask permission to cross a runway or go direct to a fix; a proper clearance or instruction is one that tells you explicitly what to do, not one that just "okays" what you proposed.

Go around: Instructions for a pilot to abandon an approach to landing. Additional instructions may follow. When told to go around, a pilot on an IFR flight plan making an instrument approach should execute the published missed approached procedure or proceed as instructed by ATC.

Have numbers: Used by pilots to inform ATC that they have received runway, wind, and altimeter information for a destination airport. Sometimes requested by ATC—e.g., "Advise when you have numbers."

Hold for release: Used by ATC to delay a departing aircraft for traffic management reasons (weather, traffic volume, etc.). Such instructions are used to inform a pilot or controller that a departure clearance is not valid until a release time or until additional instructions are received.

Ident: A request for a pilot to activate the aircraft transponder's identification, or Ident, feature. This helps a controller identify an aircraft or reconfirm an identification.

Maintain: (1) When used in reference to altitude or flight level, this term means you should remain at the altitude/flight level specified. The phrase "climb and" or "descend and" normally precedes "maintain" and the altitude assignment; e.g., "Descend and maintain five thousand feet." (2) In other ATC instructions, the term is used in its literal sense—e.g., "Maintain VFR."

Make short approach: Tells the pilot to alter the traffic pattern so as to make a short final approach. This is used to maintain separation if other aircraft are inbound for landing. ATC offers this instruction only to VFR traffic.

Mayday: The international radio distress signal (from the French "*m'aider*" ("Help me"). When repeated three times, it indicates imminent and grave danger and requests immediate assistance. (See PAN-PAN)

Minimum En route IFR Altitude (MEA): The lowest published altitude between radio fixes that assures acceptable navigational signal coverage and meets obstacle clearance requirements between those fixes. The MEA prescribed for a federal airway or segment thereof, area navigation low or high route, or other direct route applies to the entire width of the airway, segment, or route between the fixes defining it.

Negative: "No," or "Permission not granted,"or "That is not correct."

Negative contact: Used by pilots to inform ATC that: (1) Previously issued traffic is not in sight. The pilot may then request a controller's assistance in avoiding the traffic. Pilots frequently respond to traffic notices with "Looking" (which means "I'm looking, and I don't see it"); or "No joy" (a military term which means the pilot doesn't see the traffic, so there is no joy in the cockpit). Either of these two is adequate, but the preferred response is still "Negative contact." (2) The pilot was unable to contact ATC on a particular assigned frequency.

Numerous targets vicinity (location): This is a traffic advisory issued by ATC to advise pilots that targets on the radar scope near a given location are too numerous to issue individually.

Over: My transmission is ended; I expect a response." (Rarely heard in the ATC environment today.)

Pan-Pan: The international radio urgency signal. When repeated three times, indicates uncertainty or alert, followed by the nature of the urgency.

Pilot's discretion: When used in conjunction with an altitude assignment, means that ATC has offered the option of starting a climb or descent whenever you wish, and of conducting that climb or descent at any desired rate. Once the aircraft departs an altitude, however, you may not return to that altitude without another altitude assignment.

Procedure turn inbound: That point of a procedure turn maneuver where course reversal has been completed and an aircraft is established inbound on the intermediate approach segment or final approach course. A report of "procedure turn inbound" is normally used as a position report for traffic separation purposes.

Radar contact: (1) Used by ATC to inform an aircraft that it is identified on the radar display, and that radar flight following will be provided until radar identification is terminated. Radar service is provided within the limits of necessity and capability. When an aircraft is in "radar contact," the pilot automatically discontinues reporting over compulsory reporting points. (2) Used between controllers during a handoff to inform another controller that the aircraft is identified and approval is granted for the aircraft to enter the receiving controller's airspace.

Radar contact lost: Used by ATC to inform a pilot that radar identification of the aircraft has been lost. The loss may be attributed to the aircraft's merging with weather or ground clutter on radar, the aircraft's flying below the radar line of sight, the aircraft's entering an area of poor radar return, or a failure of the aircraft transponder or the ground radar equipment.

Radar service terminated: Informs a pilot that the flight will no longer be provided any of the services normally available while in radar contact. Radar service is automatically terminated, and the pilot is not advised, in the following cases: (1) an aircraft cancels its IFR flight plan (except when flying within a TCA [Terminal Control Area], ARSA [Airport Radar Service Area], etc.); (2) an aircraft conducting an instrument, visual, or contact approach has landed or has been instructed to change to advisory frequency; (3) an arriving VFR aircraft, receiving radar service, lands at a tower-controlled airport or is instructed to change to a tower or advisory frequency; or (4) an aircraft completes a radar approach.

Read back: "Repeat my message back to me."

Report: Instructs a pilot to advise ATC of a specific occurrence or condition; e.g., "Report passing Blue Ridge VOR."

Resume own navigation: Advises the pilot to resume navigational responsibility for the flight. This command is issued after completion of a radar vector or when radar contact is lost while the aircraft is being radar-vectored.

Roger: "I have received all of your last transmission." It should not be used to answer a question requiring a yes or no answer. (See p. 33.)

Runway heading: The magnetic direction indicated by the runway number. When cleared to "fly/maintain runway heading," pilots are expected to comply by flying the heading indicated by the runway number *without* applying any drift correction; e.g., Runway 4, magnetic heading 040°.

Say again: Used to request a repeat of the last transmission. Usually indicates that a transmission or portion thereof was not understood or received.

Sir/Ma'am: This term is not part of the official FAA/ATC glossary—it is merely a title of courtesy. It's not required by any written regulation, but there is a rule of civility and manners on the air observed by most professional pilots and controllers you will encounter. In most parts of the country, on any given ATC frequency, typical exchanges include such terms of respect for others when time allows. A simple phrase like "Thanks, good day" after ATC grants a request can make all the difference in whether you are perceived as a pro or a jerk (and sometimes can have an effect on whether your preferred route or altitude is made available). People like to be treated with courtesy and usually respond in kind. A pleasant demeanor on the radio indicates a professional attitude, and serves a pilot well throughout a flying career.

Stand by: Means the controller or pilot must pause for a few seconds, usually to attend to other duties of a higher priority. Also means to wait as in "Stand by for clearance." It is a grossly underused term. The FARs give pilots the right to fly the plane first, then talk on the radio. If you're too busy to copy a clearance or answer a question, "Stand by" merely asks the controller to wait briefly while you get everything in order.

TRACON (Terminal Radar Approach CONtrol): An ATC facility near a large airport that provides approach and departure control radar service to aircraft operating in and around the region surrounding the principal airport or airports. Usually referred to on the radio as "Approach" or "Departure."

Traffic in sight: Informs ATC that previously issued

traffic is in sight. Another military term, "tally ho," is a common substitute, although it's not standard FAA phraseology. (See *Negative Contact.*)

Unable: Indicates inability to comply with a specific instruction, request, or clearance. The inability may arise due to weather, traffic, equipment limitations, pilot or controller workload, or other factors.

When able: When used in conjunction with ATC instructions, gives the pilot the latitude to delay compliance until a condition or event has been reconciled. Unlike "pilot's discretion," the preface "when able" means the pilot is expected to seek the first opportunity to comply.

Wilco: This term, like many in the aviation radio lexicon, owes its origin to the military. It means "I have received your message, understand it, and will comply with it." Since it doesn't include a repeat of the transmission received, this term should not be substituted for a full readback of an important instruction or clearance.

With you: This is another unofficial but extremely common term. You use this on your initial contact with a new controller or facility frequency, but *only after a handoff to that frequency*. For example, "Oke City Approach, Cessna Four–Five–Five–X-ray *with you* at three thousand" tells the controller that you're now on the new frequency, and also says, "You should be expecting me, since I was handed off to you from someone else."

Upon hearing "With you," the controller looks for your flight information. If he doesn't have it, you've alerted him that something is amiss. In this way, just two words send a wealth of information to the controller without congesting the frequency.

CHAPTER 4

The Three Phases
of IFR Flight

A Communications Overview

The rest of this manual focuses on the various phases of IFR flight and the communications tasks that accompany each. Every phase presents different answers to the "three questions"—*Who, Why, What* (see chapter 2).

The primary difference between flying in true instrument conditions and in VFR weather is an "awareness of place." When flying in solid cloud, a pilot has no visual cues from the outside world, yet must always know exactly where the aircraft is and where it's going. Such awareness comes from flight instruments, charts, and an abstract internal "sense," perhaps best described as the ability to think in three dimensions at once. This sense depends partly upon innate ability, but mostly upon training and study.

Just as you become aware of *where* you are during a flight, you must also know *when* you are in the flight. What "phase" of the flight are you in? Are you still in the departure phase, or have you transitioned to the en route stage? Is it time to make a position report, or should you be studying the approach charts and airport diagram? Every IFR flight consists of a *departure* phase, an *en route* phase, and an *arrival* phase. Each of these three phases includes several shorter segments. Once you understand the different phases and segments, you will know what communications to expect during each. This understanding is the cornerstone for simple, consistent, predictable IFR communications.

This chapter presents an overview of the many phases and segments of IFR flight. Not every flight includes every segment described, but most flights consist of at least a few. In later chapters, each phase and segment is discussed individually, and communications requirements for each are outlined. At the end of each chapter are sample radio dialogues appropriate for the particular flight segment.

THE DEPARTURE PHASE

Filing the Flight Plan

The first flight plan you filed was probably a VFR plan that you prepared as part of your primary flight training. You drew lines on sectionals and picked out reference points for hours at a time, then painstakingly filled out the FAA flight plan form. After your instructor looked it over (and made a few improvements), you called up a briefer at the local Flight Service Station, or FSS, and filed the plan. Later, just before or after takeoff, you called Flight Service on a local frequency and opened your flight plan. After the flight (or as you approached the destination airport), you called the FSS at your destination and canceled, or closed, your flight plan.

Those days are gone. When you fly within the IFR system, flight plans are opened and closed for you by the various ground facilities watching your progress. If you depart from a controlled field, the local controller will notify the IFR system when you take off. If your flight began at an uncontrolled facility, your flight plan is activated when you contact the departure control facility on the frequency assigned. When you arrive at your destination, you can cancel IFR with the approach controller, let the control tower notify ATC when you land, or phone Flight Service yourself (if landing at an uncontrolled field).

But we're getting ahead of ourselves. Before you fly in the IFR system, you must file an IFR flight plan. Creating the plan is actually much easier than it is for VFR flight because navigational aids are only provided along certain routes. You choose your route of flight, which consists of Victor airways, segments along VOR radials, intersections of radials, RNAV or Loran direct routes, or combinations thereof. Once you've jotted down the route and analyzed the weather, calculate all the numbers for the flight plan (such as fuel on board, time en route, and true airspeed). Fill in the remaining blanks, and you're ready to contact the FAA and file the IFR flight plan.

Today, there are many ways to file an IFR flight plan with the FAA. The original standby is still available—calling the local FSS and reading your flight plan to a briefer. In addition, at most automated stations you can dial a "Fast-File" number and read the plan directly onto a recording device without waiting for a briefer to come onto the line. Other options include filing through a commercial flight planning service (in which you give your plan to someone else to file), or transmitting your flight plan directly to the FAA computer system, using one of the Direct User Access Terminal (DUAT) services or a proprietary on-line information network such as WSI, CompuServe, or Flight Data Center.

Although it is discouraged, you can also file an IFR flight plan with Flight Service (but *not* normally with ATC) while you're in the air. This may be necessary if the weather for your VFR hop turns bad. This process is time-consuming, but it's better than nothing if your alternatives are few. You establish radio contact with a nearby FSS and tell them you wish to file an IFR flight plan from your present position to your destination. The flight briefer will ask you for all the necessary information. You must maintain VFR while filing, and at all times until you receive an IFR clearance from ATC. Getting your flight plan processed and a clearance issued in this manner could take thirty minutes or more, so be sure you have enough fuel (and good enough weather) to wait.

So far, except for choosing your route of flight and deciding on an alternate destination (if required), preparing and filing an IFR flight plan seems very much like VFR flight planning. Once the flight plan is filed, however, the two paths diverge. When a flight plan is designated as IFR at the top of the form, it is entered into the FAA's computers. Your flight then becomes part of a vast scheduling network that allows many aircraft to occupy crowded airspace safely. Back when you only filed VFR flight plans, you were merely informing Flight Service of your scheduled trip. If you opened a VFR plan and then failed to close it, the system was set up to look for you along your intended route. You were saying, "Here is where I'm going, and the route I'm taking. If I haven't checked in by tonight, come looking for me."

With an IFR flight plan, however, things are different. The "route of flight" statement is actually just a *request*— the FAA decides whether your chosen route fits in with the airspace and traffic conditions for that time and location. You will be *assigned* a route, for better or worse. Sometimes, heavy IFR traffic or military activity causes the FAA to assign you a route that is far from a straight line. If this happens and the weather is good, you may want to forget the IFR plan, depart VFR instead, and just go where you want. This is the primary reason instrument-rated pilots decide against filing IFR on some clear-weather days. Flying an out-of-the-way route is an inconvenience, to be sure, but it's usually a small price to pay if your only alternative is sitting for hours on the ground in the drizzle, waiting for the skies to clear.

Picking Up the Clearance

Once the FAA schedules your flight and reserves a block of airspace with your name on it, you have to call back and find out what your assigned route is. This is called "picking up the clearance," and usually takes place on the ground, although you can pick up a clearance in the air (if you so specify in the "Remarks" section of a flight plan form). Most pilots pick up a clearance in one of two ways: by radio, using a "Clearance Delivery" frequency; or by telephone.

Depending upon where you are, the Clearance Delivery frequency may have any of several forms. At large controlled airports, it is usually one or two controllers on a special frequency used only for clearance purposes. At smaller controlled fields, you may receive your clearance from the ground controller on the normal Ground frequency, or even from the tower controller. At uncontrolled fields near large airports, you can often reach the clearance controller on the larger facility's Clearance frequency. Since you normally don't radio Clearance Delivery until you're in your airplane, the controller will request your clearance, read it to you, and inform the ATC system that you'll be departing soon. Once the tower releases you, or you contact departure on the frequency specified, your flight plan is activated.

At more remote uncontrolled fields, however, you must phone a nearby FSS or TRACON facility to get your clearance. They will give you not only the standard clearance information (clearance limit, route of flight, altitude, departure frequency, and transponder code), but also a "release time" and/or "void time." Since you are phoning from a ground facility, the clearance controller knows you aren't ready for taxi or takeoff. Therefore, you are given a brief "window" of time, usually fifteen to thirty minutes into the future, when you are released for entry into the IFR system. If you don't get off the ground before the void time, this "window" closes, and your clearance is void.

Proper techniques for getting your clearance, and getting it right, are detailed in chapter 6, "Picking Up the Clearance."

Takeoff

Whether your IFR clearance includes release and void times, or you are released for departure by a control tower, you don't officially enter the IFR system until you are airborne. After you tell the local tower you're ready for takeoff, expect a brief delay before you're cleared for departure. The tower will call the proper ATC facility and request a "release" for you into their airspace. If you are departing from an uncontrolled airport and were given a release time, the IFR release occurs automatically at that time. No delay is necessary before takeoff.

Contact Departure

After you reach a certain altitude or leave the airport traffic pattern, the tower (if there is one) will hand you off to the departure facility. When departing an uncontrolled field, you switch frequencies when you depart the pattern at the airport. You were given the proper departure frequency in the clearance, so your next call is to Departure to inform them that you've departed and are starting on the route given to you, and to report your altitude. If you are in a radar service environment, Departure will inform you when you are in radar contact.

The departure facility you first contact will be either a TRACON facility, if you are near a large airport, or the en route Center responsible for your area. TRACON facilities have fairly limited service areas, so you will eventually be handed off to the appropriate Center facility for the en route portion of the flight.

THE EN ROUTE PHASE

Handoffs

To veterans of controlled airspace, there is no particular mystery surrounding frequency handoffs. Yet there was a first time for every pilot when ATC said, "Contact Center on One–Two–Two–Point–One–Five, good day." There you were, engaged in friendly cooperation with the local Center, when without warning they dumped you. You changed the frequency, listened for a break, and called the controller. What a relief it was when another voice not only answered, but actually knew who you were and where you were going.

This ritual is known as the "handoff." As the name implies, it's a planned exchange between controllers in which responsibility for your flight, and voice communication with you, pass from one person to another. It's not as if a controller tosses you aside, leaving you to your own devices in the IFR system. On the contrary, it's a coordinated transfer of control from one sector to another (if within the same Center facility), or between two different facilities.

When a flight plan enters the IFR system, the FAA's computers transmit data about your flight to every control facility along your route. This data arrives at each facility shortly before a given aircraft is scheduled to arrive in the area, and is printed on a thin strip of paper. This data strip for a flight lists the type and ID of the aircraft, altitude and route assignments, and other information. Using these data strips, controllers keep a running list of aircraft within their areas. Once the aircraft departs the area or lands, that flight's data strip is set aside and replaced with those for other arriving aircraft.

Here is a sample handoff: Suppose you are approaching Oklahoma City on an IFR flight plan, flying northwest toward Denver. When you arrive in the Oklahoma City area, Fort Worth Center (an en route ARTCC facility) contacts Oklahoma City Approach (a TRACON facility) by telephone to request a handoff. Approach knew you were coming—they received a data strip on you fifteen minutes ago. Approach identities you on radar, and accepts your flight from Center. Center calls your aircraft and tells you to "Contact Oke City Approach on One–One–Niner–Point–Three, good day." You acknowledge the frequency, switch over, and call Approach. Lo and behold, the controller is expecting you, and you're greeted with an altimeter setting or possibly a vector.

The above is a fairly typical handoff scenario, in which

you call an entirely new facility as you depart the control area of another. Upon leaving the area controlled by Oke City Approach, you will likely be handed right back to Fort Worth Center, but on a different Center frequency than before. Some handoffs are made between controllers in one facility, as you travel from one sector to another. In fact, the handoff may occur between two controllers who are seated next to each other at their consoles.

"Wait a minute," you say. "In your example, why did I call an approach facility in Oklahoma City if I was en route to another city?" Good question. The answer illustrates the importance of knowing both *where* and *when* you are in your flight. Even though you're in the en route phase of the flight, you still may be controlled by approach or departure facilities if you travel within their airspace. In fact, on a short IFR flight between airports in one general area, you may talk *only* to the local TRACON, and never to an en route Center facility at all. This is because the en route phase is so short that you never leave the airspace controlled by the TRACON. Regardless of *whom* you're calling, however, radio communications with each facility are basically the same when you're en route.

Compulsory Reporting Points (Non-Radar En Route)

In populated areas of the country, most IFR flights today take place within the radar environment—that is, by flying at or above the Minimum En route Altitude (MEA) along your route, you will be in radar contact with ATC throughout the flight. This permits ATC to watch your progress continuously, with a clear picture of your position, heading, ground speed, and altitude (if you have a Mode C- or

Mode S-equipped transponder). The primary advantage of this radar coverage is obvious—ATC can best steer and control that which it can see.

Yet in many parts of the United States, the IFR system can, and often does, operate without radar coverage over great areas. Even in areas where radar is normally available, coverage can be lost if equipment malfunctions or if an aircraft operates too low. The system still works in this situation, although ATC must rely on the pilot to make regular "position reports" in order to protect the airspace around the flight.

Ordinarily, upon contacting the first departure facility named in your clearance, you will be greeted with the statement, "radar contact." From that point forward, you will continue to be in radar contact unless a controller advises you later that radar contact was lost. Whenever your flight is *not* in radar contact, you must make position reports to an appropriate facility any time you reach a fix specified by the controller (e.g., a VOR or intersection) or a compulsory reporting point as shown on the en route charts. Position reports include your current position and altitude, the time you reached that fix, your next reporting point, your estimated time of arrival at that next point, and the name of the next succeeding fix.

Sometimes, radar coverage goes out of service in a given area, and a controller will name one or two reporting fixes. You are to notify ATC when you reach the specified points. When the radar equipment comes back on line, or you travel back into an active radar area, the controller will notify you that your aircraft is once again "radar contact," that is, it is visible and identified on radar. At this time, you should discontinue the position reports unless radar contact is lost again.

Revised Clearances

Anytime ATC changes an assigned altitude, expands a clearance limit, issues a vector, or otherwise alters the clearance you originally received, you have received a "revised clearance." Each revised clearance *replaces* prior clearances, but only for the items it affects. For example, you are climbing through 9,000 feet to your assigned altitude of 17,000 and you've been cleared direct to the Kiowa (Colorado) VORTAC, then on course. If Denver Center calls and instructs you to climb and maintain flight level 220 (22,000 feet), then that is your new assigned altitude. The clearance has been "revised," but as to altitude only. You are not to level off at 17,000 feet, but instead should continue to flight level 220. You *do*, however, continue direct to Kiowa and then on course. Center didn't change your *route* in the revised clearance, so you go where you were originally cleared.

Conversely, suppose in the above example you received the higher altitude assignment, then two minutes later were told, "Fly heading One–Two–Zero, upon receiving Hugo, proceed direct Hugo then on course." *Now* your route has changed. You still proceed to the higher altitude (since these new instructions didn't mention altitude), but now you won't go to Kiowa at all—you fly the heading assigned, and as soon as you receive the Hugo VORTAC, you fly directly there.

It is indeed the rare clearance that doesn't vary at least a bit from the route requested. When you file for a specific route at a specific time of day, chances are ATC will have to vary the request a bit in order to shoehorn your flight into existing traffic. Typically, a clearance includes some vectoring or perhaps a trip to an intersection that's off the direct flight path. Later, after departure, you may only be halfway to that intersection when ATC revises your clearance, telling you that you may now turn on course to join your preferred route. Contrary to popular opinion, ATC doesn't alter your clearance, then revise it back to the route you filed, just to be obnoxious. Your requested route of flight was likely in the path of some existing traffic, so your clearance routed you around that path. When that traffic is no longer a factor, then ATC will ordinarily steer you back onto your requested route as expeditiously as possible.

It is also the rare flight in which a clearance isn't *revised* at least once or twice. The most common revisions involve altitude steps during climb or descent, and vectors during departure or approach. A revised clearance may come at any time, yet another reason to have pencil and paper within reach at all times during the flight. If the revision is a complex one, most controllers will tip you off by telling you they have a revised clearance and that you should "advise when ready to copy." This is the warning signal that you're about to copy a whole new routing. Regardless of its complexity, however, a revised clearance usually means little major work on your part. If you have the proper charts at hand in the aircraft, you need only look at the new route, set your nav equipment appropriately, and fly the airplane.

Going Off Frequency

During the flight, you will occasionally need to call some other radio facility for information, assistance, or to report your position or the weather. Unless your flight crew consists of two, this means you have to change frequencies. Breaking contact with ATC means disrupting the very thing which makes the IFR system work—communications. Therefore, you should avoid leaving your assigned frequency unless (*a*) it's really necessary; (*b*) you request (and receive) permission to leave the frequency; and (*c*) you take care of whatever business you have and reestablish contact with ATC as soon as possible.

Anticipating Your Arrival

Before the end of the en route phase of a flight, think ahead to the arrival phase. As you near your destination, ATC will clear you to lower altitudes and put you on the initial approach course. By the time you are descending into rougher air in solid clouds, it's too late to start rummaging around in the flight bag looking for approach plates and your stopwatch. You should spend the last portion of level cruise flight anticipating and planning the approach and landing.

Begin by pulling any needed STAR (Standard Terminal ARrival) charts and the approach charts appropriate to your intended destination. Using your number two comm radio (if your aircraft is so equipped), or after receiving permission from ATC to go off frequency, monitor the ATIS broadcast for your destination (or a major facility near it). By getting an idea of the local conditions while you're still far away from the airport, you can anticipate the weather, the surface winds, the approach to expect, and the preferred runway(s).

Consult the en route chart for your present position, and visualize the expected flight path to your destination. This final "chart check" will help you navigate intuitively when things get busy during the arrival phase of your flight.

THE ARRIVAL PHASE

Approach Control

As you near your destination, the last controller who works your flight (except for those actually on the airport, e.g., tower and ground control) will be the *approach* controller. Near most large airports, a local TRACON facility provides approach and departure services. When using the radio, you refer to a TRACON as "Approach" or "Departure," depending upon the phase of flight you're in. This designation differs from the "Center" designation given to an ARTCC.

For example, Kansas City Center (an ARTCC) handles en route IFR traffic in northeastern Oklahoma, but you call Tulsa Approach (a TRACON) if you're landing at Tulsa International. Likewise, Denver Center is the ARTCC in charge of most of Colorado, but Denver *Approach* is a TRACON, separate from Denver Center, that controls departures and arrivals in and around the city.

If your destination is more remote, the en route Center controller may also be your approach controller. In this situation, you still say "Center" when talking to the facility, even though the controller provides approach control services.

The approach controller's job is to help you transition from en route flight to the approach. Ordinarily, your flight is cleared to descend to an appropriate altitude, then vectored into position at an initial or intermediate approach fix. Finally, you are cleared for the approach and told when to change frequencies for the tower or advisory frequency at your destination. If your destination has no control tower, the approach controller will instruct you to call back on a specified approach frequency in the event of a missed approach.

Cancel IFR?

At any time during an IFR flight, you may cancel your IFR flight plan merely by informing the controller in charge of your flight. A pilot may only cancel IFR if the aircraft is in VFR conditions, and the pilot must maintain VFR once the flight plan is canceled.

Typically, a pilot only cancels IFR when (*a*) the aircraft has descended into VFR conditions at an initial approach altitude, (*b*) the pilot has the airport in sight, and (*c*) the destination airport is an uncontrolled field. If the airport has a control tower and is in VFR conditions, an approach controller can clear the flight for a "visual" approach, and then hand the pilot off to the tower. Once the aircraft lands, the tower controller notifies Approach and the IFR flight plan is automatically canceled.

If the airport is uncontrolled, however, the pilot must either cancel IFR with the approach controller, or telephone Flight Service (or ATC) after landing to "close" the flight plan (much like closing a VFR flight plan). Since the approach controller is responsible for tracking an IFR flight (and maintaining aircraft separation) until the pilot cancels IFR or lands, it is easier for the controller if the pilot can safely cancel IFR before landing.

Just as you have the right to cancel your flight plan, you also have the right to demand a full approach even in VFR conditions. If you're flying in good weather, with the airport in sight, and you're familiar with the area, there is usually no reason not to cancel IFR with the approach controller. Doing so reduces the pressure on the controller a little bit, and you'll be the good guy. If, on the other hand, you're unfamiliar with the destination airport, or if haze or a low sun restricts visibility, it's usually safer to request a full approach to the airport. Shooting a published approach gives you navigational cues that confirm what your eyes tell you—that you really are near the right airport or lined up on the proper runway.

ATC automatically closes any IFR flight plan if: (1) the pilot cancels IFR; or (2) the aircraft lands at a controlled field after an instrument, visual, or contact approach.

Cleared for the Approach

Once the approach controller steers you to the proper altitude and position, you will be cleared for some type of approach to the destination airport. If the weather is good, you probably will have been warned to "Expect visual approach, Runway XX." If clouds obscure your view of the runway, you will be set up for an instrument approach (or a contact approach, if available). When you are at the proper position and altitude, the controller will issue a final set of instructions; e.g., "You are one mile from the outer marker, maintain three thousand until established on the localizer, cleared for the ILS Runway Three–One Left, contact the tower now, One–One–Eight–Point–One." At this point, follow the instructions in a logical order. First (since ATC said "now"), you contact the tower and continue to maintain 3,000 feet. When the localizer needle shows signs of life, turn onto the inbound heading and track the signal. Once you are established inbound on the localizer, your clearance to start the approach takes effect. You are cleared to execute the published approach, and if the tower okays it, to land.

The IFR flight ends just as it began—with the aircraft rolling down the runway. While you still have radio calls to make as you taxi to park, they are not segments of the IFR flight. When your wheels hit the ground and you turn off the active runway, your IFR flight is over.

PART TWO

Departure Communications

CHAPTER 5

Filing an IFR Flight Plan

The first step in a precise, predictable IFR flight is getting your flight plan filed correctly. It does little good for you to hone your instrument navigation and radio skills if you can't tell ATC where you want to go in the first place, since a perfect IFR flight is of no use if you get routed to the wrong destination.

Arguably, the most accurate way to file flight plans is by direct hookup into the FAA's computer system. Because computer technology is changing so rapidly, this manual cannot attempt to teach proper use of the many on-line data options available for flight plan filing. Most systems operate via a telephone link with the pilot's personal computer or with a leased terminal at an FBO. The pilot fills out a flight plan form on the computer screen, then transmits the plan directly to the FAA over the phone line. Without a doubt, the introduction of on-line filing, especially DUAT services, has forever changed the face of flight plan filing.

No matter how sophisticated hardware becomes, however, there will be times when a pilot must rely on voice communications (via telephone or radio) to file a flight plan. You will eventually find yourself at a remote location, with no laptop computer, no fixed terminal at the airport, and no way to upload a flight plan by direct computer hookup. When this happens, it's time to contact a Flight Service Station for filing—just as pilots have done for decades.

The act of reading your flight plan over the phone or radio to another person (or to a Fast-File recorder) sets the stage for error by every person involved in the process. First, you read your flight plan aloud. Someone then has to transcribe it; then it is entered into a computer. Each of these steps has the potential for human error. For example, you might get something slightly wrong in the original flight plan (such as miscalculating the Zulu time value for your estimated time of departure). The Flight Service specialist could misspell the three-letter identifier for an en route fix when transcribing the flight plan. The possibilities for error or omission are endless, and the consequences can range from a slight inconvenience to disaster. When you file through Flight Service, therefore, you should do all you can to minimize the chance of a communications error in filing your flight plan.

None of this is to say that the file-with-a-briefer system is necessarily any less accurate than filing directly, or that computers are infallible. But computers today are fundamentally reliable, and the FAA's computer system operates like most—"garbage in, garbage out," that is, their computers can only work with what goes into them. If incorrect data is entered with the flight plan, the computer issues an incorrect flight plan. It doesn't matter who is at fault for the erroneous information, the result is still in-accurate.

When you do file with a briefer, then, take the time to do it right. Even though the only communications factor within your control is yourself, you can improve accuracy in the filing process by communicating your flight plan to Flight Service clearly and accurately. Whether you use a radio or telephone, the following rules apply for transmitting your flight plan:

- *Write everything down ahead of time.* Pilots who don't fill out a flight plan form may forget to calculate important numbers (such as time en route or true airspeed), or may file incorrect routings. If you don't mention your estimated time en route, for example, the briefer will ask for that information. If you forgot to calculate the time beforehand, using forecast or reported winds aloft, you'll be forced to guess at the en route time—and your guess could cause you to run short of fuel if the winds turn out to be stronger than you expected.

  If you don't have a flight plan form available, calculate as much information as possible for your flight before you call Flight Service. Again, write everything down, especially your route of flight (with three-letter identifiers) and the important numbers: fuel on board, time en route, and true airspeed. Just inform the briefer that you don't have a flight plan form in front of you, and you'll be asked for each bit of information in order.

- *Speak slowly and clearly.* The flight plan is the first component of the IFR flight, so clear speech is as important now as it is when you're cleared for takeoff. Resist the temptation to speak rapidly or softly. Slow down, speak up, and overpronounce any words that could be misunderstood.

• *Use the phonetic alphabet for identifiers.* Every pilot should know the approved phonetic alphabet for radio communications (see Appendix). When you read the flight plan to a briefer, use phonetic spellings of any really vital information, such as the three-letter identifiers for VORs and airports.

• *Use both the name and identifier for all airports.* When reading the name of an en route fix, such as a VORTAC or intersection, give the identifier *only*. Many airports, on the other hand, have the same identifier as a nearby VOR, so give the identifier *and name* of any departure or destination airports to avoid confusion.

For example, Denver's Stapleton International Airport has the three-letter identifier DEN. The same identifier represents the DEN VORTAC located on the field at that airport. If you were flying from the CYS VORTAC (Cheyenne, Wyoming), over Denver, to the COS VORTAC (Colorado Springs, Colorado) on low-altitude Victor airways, your flight plan would include the route "CYS–V19–DEN–V81–COS." You would read this portion of the route to the briefer as "Charlie–Yankee–Sierra, Victor One–Niner, Delta–Echo–November, Victor Eight–One, Charlie–Oscar–Sierra." The Delta–Echo–November identifier informs the briefer that you are merely navigating via the DEN VORTAC, and that Stapleton Airport is not on your flight plan.

If, on the other hand, you wish to fly to Denver's Stapleton *and land there,* your destination would read "STAPLETON DEN." This is read aloud as "Stapleton Delta–Echo–November." By using the full name of the airport, you tell the briefer that the airport, and not the VORTAC, is your fix.

Users of more sophisticated navigational equipment are used to seeing a "K" precede the identifier of all airports. For example, DEN is the Denver VORTAC, while KDEN is Stapleton Airport. Using this type of identifier when filing the flight plan will usually work (i.e., the Flight Service folks will understand what you're requesting), but it's still good insurance against errors to use both the airport name and identifier when filing.

• *Read the headings.* Someone has to copy your flight plan information onto a form (or into a computer). To be sure you and the briefer are looking at the same information, it helps if you read the *headings* of the flight plan form as you go along. For example, when reading the proposed route of flight, say the words, "Route of flight" and then give the route. Do the same for each item on the form. If you're leaving anything blank, you should say so. Otherwise, the briefer may think you forgot (e.g., if you're not specifying an alternate airport, say, "Alternate airport, none").

• *Tips for Fast-File users*: If you operate from an area serviced by a larger, automated Flight Service Station, you will undoubtedly come into contact with Fast-File sooner or later. Fast-File is basically a telephone answering machine that you can dial directly or access from a Main Menu of telephone services. After hearing a brief message and a beep tone, you read your flight plan onto the recording and hang up. A Flight Service briefer will listen to the tape, transcribe the flight plan, and enter it into the FAA's system. This process takes anywhere from fifteen to sixty minutes, depending on the workload at the station. It is therefore advisable to file as early as possible on the day of (or the day before) a flight.

When speaking to the Fast-File recorder, remember to speak slowly. Someone has to listen to your message and copy down all the information. The recorder won't interrupt you, ask you to repeat a portion of the flight plan, or remind you of an item you omitted. It is doubly important, then, that you give complete, accurate information when using Fast-File. In order to simplify the transcription process, be sure to read the headings as outlined above.

Finally, it's advisable to leave the area code and phone number you're calling from when using Fast-File, and to state how long you can be reached at that number. Leaving a contact phone number is extra insurance against confusion—if you omitted any essential information or if something you said is garbled, Flight Service can call you for clarification. Give the number after you finish reading the flight plan and just say, "I can be reached at the following phone number until (time)."

You should be able to use Fast-File without problems if you remember these three rules: (*a*) file early, (*b*) speak clearly, and (*c*) leave your phone number.

If the foregoing makes flight plan filing seem complicated, don't worry; it isn't. It is, however, important. The above "rules" are really just matters of common sense and/or experience. By taking a few extra steps when you file your flight plan, you can save yourself considerable aggravation, and reduce the risk of a communications breakdown before your aircraft ever leaves the ground.

CHAPTER 6

Picking Up the Clearance

Now that your flight plan is on file with the FAA, you must again contact them in order to receive your clearance. Without a clearance, you cannot operate in instrument weather conditions or within controlled airspace. By filing the flight plan, you tell ATC that you expect to make a particular flight. Until you pick up your clearance and activate it, however, you are still not operating within the IFR system.

As discussed in chapter 4, you can pick up your clearance by telephone or radio. If you are departing from an uncontrolled field and no Clearance Delivery frequency is available, you must telephone the nearest Flight Service Station or FAA control facility and request your clearance. This contact requires little explanation—you phone the facility a few minutes before engine start, tell the specialist that you wish to pick up an IFR clearance, and the FAA will take it from there. Your only worries are copying the clearance accurately (see p. 75), reading it back, and departing before your void time.

If, on the other hand, you call for your clearance by radio, it's an occasion for applying the "three questions" principle of radio communications. That is, before you call on the Clearance Delivery frequency, ask yourself *whom* you are talking to, *why* you are calling them, and *what* they want to know from you when you call. The answers to these questions will dictate what you should say on the air. The appropriate time to call for the clearance is *after* you're aboard the aircraft, and either right before or right after engine start. Clearance delivery expects you to be ready to taxi within a few minutes, because they are about to notify ATC that you're on your way into the system. If you fly a piston aircraft, calling right after engine start allows a few minutes for warmup while you wait for the clearance. Turbine equipment, however, burns fuel very quickly on the ground, and needs little, if any, warming up; so it's best to finish all pre-start chores and copy the clearance before starting the engines.

WHOM Am I Talking To?

You're contacting the controller in charge of *clearance delivery*. At larger airports, furnishing clearances is this controller's only job (apart from recording ATIS information), and there is a discrete frequency used only for clearance delivery. At many smaller controlled fields, the ground or tower controllers double as the clearance controller. Sometimes, a clearance controller at a major airport provides clearance delivery services to neighboring satellite airports if radio range permits.*

Regardless of who receives your call, however, it is clearance delivery service that you are requesting. In your initial contact, you will tell them this.

WHY Am I Calling Them?

You are calling the clearance controller to request the IFR clearance which (you hope) the FAA has stored for you in its computers. You cannot file (or modify) a flight plan with this controller, nor can you request permission to taxi or to depart. You are merely calling to say, "Please pick up my clearance from the FAA and read it to me. Be sure I read it back to you correctly, then advise the ATC system that I will be departing soon."

WHAT Will They Want to Know When I Call?

In order to call up your clearance from the FAA computer, the controller must know: (1) who you are (your aircraft ID); (2) whether you are VFR or IFR; and (3) where you are going. The VFR/IFR distinction is only necessary if you're departing from an airport in or near a TCA or ARSA, in which case you'll need a clearance to depart VFR as well as IFR. A proper radio call will provide all this information to the clearance controller in one brief sentence. The controller will ask for any further information if needed.

* In some areas, you can also reach a FSS from the ground through an RCO (Remote Communications Outlet). RCO frequencies are shown on VFR sectionals and IFR en route charts.

Sample Radio Calls

1. When clearance delivery is provided at the departure airport, simply state whom you're calling (here, clearance delivery at Dallas/Fort Worth), who you are (aircraft ID), whether you're IFR, and where you're going (destination airport):

DFW CLEARANCE, TWIN CESSNA THREE–EIGHT–NINER–KILO–BRAVO, IFR TO NASHVILLE, REQUEST CLEARANCE.

2. If you're calling from an uncontrolled field near a large airport, but the large airport's clearance controller handles calls for the entire area, then the call is nearly the same as above. You must, however, also state *where* you are calling from:

DFW CLEARANCE, TWIN CESSNA THREE–EIGHT–NINER–KILO–BRAVO, *AT ARLINGTON,* IFR TO NASHVILLE, REQUEST CLEARANCE.

3. If you're picking up your clearance while in flight (which you normally can't do unless you requested this in the "Remarks" section of your flight plan), you will call the TRACON or ARTCC responsible for your present location instead of calling clearance delivery. Tell them who and where you are, and what you want:

FORT WORTH CENTER, TWIN CESSNA THREE–EIGHT–NINER–KILO–BRAVO, VFR OVER SCURRY VORTAC AT SEVEN THOUSAND FIVE HUNDRED, HAVE FILED FOR IFR TO NASHVILLE, REQUEST CLEARANCE.

What to Expect in Response

The clearance controller will sometimes respond immediately with your clearance (so you'd better have pen and paper ready). Otherwise, the first response is an acknowledgment of your call and a statement that your clearance has been requested from the local ATC facility:

TWIN CESSNA NINER–KILO–BRAVO, ROGER, CLEARANCE IS ON REQUEST.

If this controller doubles as a ground controller, you may be asked if you're ready to taxi while you wait for your clearance. If you are ready, it saves time (and fuel) if you can taxi to the run-up area during the wait.

After a short delay (if it takes too long, call again), the controller will call back and ask if you're ready to copy the clearance. If you're taxiing (or otherwise occupied), politely ask the controller to stand by. If you're stopped and ready, call back, identify yourself, and say, "Ready to copy."

The Elements of an IFR Clearance

The clearance begins with your aircraft identification. If the controller reads someone else's call numbers, or reads yours incorrectly, jot down the discrepancy and point it out after the clearance has been read. The rest of the clearance will be a long, fast-paced string of instructions, frequencies, and squawk codes. The best way to copy a clearance is to use a set of abbreviations and figures, a sort of pilot's shorthand. You'll find the ability to quickly copy instructions very useful throughout an IFR flight, but nowhere so useful as when copying the full route clearance before departure (see "Copying Clearances," p. 75).

Most clearances follow the same format. This is helpful, because it's easier to copy information down if you are expecting it in a certain order. The standard clearance format is CRAFT:

C = Clearance limit (how far you are cleared to go)
R = Route (how you are supposed to get there)
A = Altitudes (initial and expected higher altitudes)
F = Frequency (departure control)
T = Transponder (discrete squawk code for your flight)

Here is a sample clearance in the CRAFT format:

TWIN CESSNA THREE–EIGHT–NINER–KILO–BRAVO CLEARED TO LITTLE ROCK ADAMS FIELD, VIA AFTER DEPARTURE TURN RIGHT HEADING ZERO–THREE–ZERO, RADAR VECTORS KMART INTERSECTION, THEN AS FILED. MAINTAIN FOUR THOUSAND, EXPECT NINER THOUSAND ONE–ZERO MINUTES AFTER DEPARTURE. DEPARTURE FREQUENCY ONE–TWO–FOUR–POINT–THREE, SQUAWK TWO–SIX–FOUR–TWO.

The *clearance limit* is the farthest fix or point along your route to which you are cleared. The controller, after stating your aircraft tail number, said, "CLEARED TO LITTLE ROCK . . ." and then gave you the routing. In this case, Little Rock is the clearance limit. Ordinarily, you'll be cleared to your destination airport—but not always. Occasionally, you're only cleared as far as some VOR or intersection along the route, and then receive further clearance along the way. The clearance limit is especially important to know if you lose two-way communications during the flight (see chapter 16 for detailed communications-failure procedures).

The *route* will sometimes be a simple "cleared as filed." For this reason, you must always have a copy of your filed route with you, in case that's the route you're cleared to fly. Otherwise, the route will typically include some vectors to a nearby fix (to get you out of local traffic), then on to your destination. In our example, you were cleared "VIA AFTER DEPARTURE TURN RIGHT HEADING ZERO–THREE–ZERO, RADAR VECTORS KMART IN-TERSECTION, THEN AS FILED." After takeoff, you will fly the vector given, and expect vectors to KMART inter-section. Upon reaching KMART you join the route you filed originally at the nearest available point. This usually means joining an airway or flying direct to the next VOR (or other fix) in your planned route.

Occasionally you will receive a completely new route, including Victor airways and VORs you've never heard of. If this happens (and you're sure the clearance is meant for you, i.e., it contains your tail number and leads to your intended destination), don't worry—just copy it down. Don't complain about the route to the clearance controller, because Clearance Delivery can't change your route for you. Better to depart on the clearance given, and then beg ATC for a shorter routing after you're established en route.

Altitudes given in your clearance are for your initial climbout and your next expected altitude. As in the exam-ple, you receive an altitude restriction and a higher alti-tude to expect within a certain time (usually ten minutes). The higher altitude will be either the cruise altitude you filed for or another step toward that cruise altitude, if traffic conditions require you to make a gradual climb.

The *frequency* given in the clearance is the first *Departure*

Control frequency for your flight. When departing from a terminal area, the frequency will be one of the TRACON's local approach/departure frequencies. If you're taking off from a more remote location, it will be the local Center frequency for the ARTCC in charge of that area. This controller expects to hear from you (and has you in radar contact, usually), after you take off and climb away from the airport.

Finally, the *transponder code* is the discrete squawk code assigned to your flight. Under normal circumstances, you will squawk that same code from takeoff to landing. This differs from VFR flight following or radar service near a terminal, in which you're given a temporary squawk code while in the service area, then told to squawk 1200 after the controller is finished with your flight.

If your flight originates at an airport not served by a control tower, the controller will finish the clearance by giving you a "release time" and a "void time" for the clearance. You will then be instructed whom to notify if you do not depart during this interval. You are not released for entry into the system until the release time, and you must depart before your void time or your clearance is void and you must call again for a new clearance (or cancel the flight plan).

Whenever a void time passes and the flight has not yet departed, do *not* depart until you notify ATC. *Never* wait more than thirty minutes beyond your void time before notifying ATC that you are still on the ground. ATC assumes you departed as planned, unless they hear otherwise. Failure to call back and tell them you haven't departed may result in ATC's rerouting or delaying other IFR traffic along your route (for a flight that was never in the air). Moreover, if you accept a clearance and then no one hears from you, ATC may initiate search-and-rescue operations to locate your aircraft.

Copying Clearances

The IFR clearance contains a lot of information, all of it essential to a safe flight. You must copy down everything the controller tells you to do, and copy it correctly. The keys to becoming a skilled clearance copier are: (1) lots of practice using symbols and abbreviations; and (2) writing down everything you hear without thinking about what it means or otherwise trying to make sense of it.

For example, suppose the clearance includes complicated instructions to fly some heading until reaching a VOR, then outbound on some radial to an intersection you never heard of—don't think about it, and don't try to visualize the flight or remember where that intersection is. By the time you stop to think about such matters, the controller has finished reading the whole clearance and you've missed the altitudes, departure frequency, and squawk code. You'll have plenty of time to consult the charts and tune your nav radios after copying the clearance. Just get the vectors, radials, and frequencies on paper—worry about how to fly the route later.

Figure 6.1 is a set of suggested abbreviations and symbols to help you copy clearances faster, using less space. This list is not exhaustive, but includes a few common abbreviations for some of the most widely used clearance terms. You may wish to adopt a few of these ideas, or you may prefer to come up with your own. It doesn't matter how you write down clearance information, so long as you write it down correctly (and can read what you write).

Figure 6.2 shows how to apply some of the symbols and

Airport	APT	Flight Level	FL
After	AFT or $\bar{p}$	Heading	HDG
Altitudes (1,000; 7,500; 10,000)	10; 75; 100	Intersection	Δ
Approach	APCH	Left	Ⓛ
At	@	Turn Left	ⓉⓁ
Above	ABV or ↗	Right	Ⓡ
At or Above	@/ABV	Turn Right	ⓉⓇ
Before	B4 or $\bar{a}$	Localizer	LOC
Below	BLO or ↘	Maintain	M
At or Below	@/BLO	Marker	MKR
Cleared	C	Over	OVR
Cleared as Filed	CAF	Procedure Turn	PT
Climb	↑	Radar Vectors	RV
Climb and Maintain	↑M	Radial (number)	(*)R
Cross	X	Report	RPT
Departure	DEP	Runway	RY
Descend	↓	Squawk	SWK
Descend and Maintain	↓M	Takeoff	T/0
Direct	Đ→	Tower	TWR
Established	EST	Via	V:
Expect	XP	VOR	Ⓥ
Expect Further Clearance	EFC	VORTAC	ⓋⓉ

Figure 6.1

Suggested abbreviations and symbols for copying IFR clearances.

abbreviations from Figure 6.1 to the sample clearance given above. When copied by the pilot, the clearance to Little Rock might look like this:

N389KB C LIT APT V:
AFT DEP ⓉⓇ HDG 030° RV KMART △,
CAF. M20, XP 90 AFT 10.
124.3   2642

Figure 6.2
Sample clearance to Little Rock using symbols from figure 6.1.

The best way to improve your clearance-copying skills is to *practice*. One way is to monitor—and copy clearances from—a nearby clearance delivery frequency during your spare time. If you don't have access to such a frequency (or the equipment needed to hear it), try one of the many practice tapes available from most mail-order suppliers or pilot shops.

Reading Back a Clearance

The FAA does not require a pilot to repeat a clearance back to a controller unless that controller specifically requests it. Common sense, however, demands a readback of *all* vital flight information, and that includes your IFR clearance. After you copy the clearance, you must read back enough information so that the controller knows you have it right—but that doesn't mean reading it back verbatim. It's possible for your readback to be too detailed, in which case you tie up the frequency. Instead, try repeating just the CRAFT items without trying to make complete sentences. Refer to the clearance in Figure 6.2, for example. That clearance might be read back as follows:

> TWIN CESSNA THREE–EIGHT–NINER–KILO–
> BRAVO CLEARED LITTLE ROCK ADAMS. AF-
> TER DEPARTURE ZERO–THREE–ZERO
> VECTORS KMART, THEN AS FILED. MAINTAIN
> FOUR THOUSAND, EXPECT NINER AFTER TEN.
> ONE–TWO–FOUR–POINT–THREE, TWO–SIX–
> FOUR–TWO.

Notice that the readback omits excess words. You needn't say the words "departure frequency," "squawk," or other obvious items to the clearance controller. You may also read it back a little faster than you'd normally speak, because the controller won't be copying the clearance from you but will just refer to the information on the printout; you need merely show that you have the numbers right. If the controller needs you to repeat part of the readback, you'll be asked to do so. Otherwise, if you read it back correctly, you'll hear:

> NINER–KILO–BRAVO, YOUR READBACK IS
> CORRECT.

Preparing for Departure

Once you have the clearance copied and read back, finish any other ground checks you may have, verify that you still have current information from the ATIS or Unicom, and then taxi for takeoff. This step is the same in IFR or VFR conditions—you merely call on the proper Ground Control (or advisory) frequency, identify your aircraft, and state your intentions or request:

> GROUND CONTROL, TWIN CESSNA THREE–
> EIGHT–NINER–KILO–BRAVO AT THE TERMI-
> NAL WITH CLEARANCE AND [ATIS identifier],
> READY TO TAXI TO ACTIVE RUNWAY.

When the controller clears you to taxi, read back any important items, such as the route you are to take ("Taxi via Charlie to Runway One–Seven") or any special instructions ("Hold short of taxiway Hotel").

One aspect of Ground Control and its authority should be known to every pilot, but bears repeating: a taxi clearance to a particular location on the airfield automatically clears you to cross any taxiways or runways along that route. The wise pilot, however, always looks carefully before crossing any intersection or runway. After all, you never know when someone—maybe even you—is taxiing in the wrong place. "See and avoid" is a good policy for your ground operations as well as for when you're airborne.

Once you are positioned near the departure runway, you are ready to complete the run-up, review the before-takeoff checklist, glance at your charts, look at the windsock, and take a deep breath. This is the last really relaxed time you'll have until you are established on cruise climb, well away from the airport. You are about to become rather busy with takeoff and departure chores, including communications. In addition, immediately after departure you face the transition between the departure and en route phases of the flight.

CHAPTER 7

Takeoff and Departure

Takeoff from a Controlled Airport

When you depart from an airport with a control tower, your IFR flight plan isn't activated—and you cannot take off—until the tower gets the go-ahead from ATC to release you. When you notify the tower that you are ready to go, the tower controller holds you on the ground and phones ATC to request a release for you. Once ATC approves the release, the tower clears you for takeoff (traffic permitting) and your IFR flight is underway.

In deciding what to say when you call the tower, just employ the "three questions": *Whom* are you calling? *Why* are you calling? and *What* do they want to know? The *whom* is easy—you're calling the tower controller, the person who has the responsibility for all traffic departing from and arriving at the runways at the airport as well as any others within the airport traffic area. Ground Control can clear you to *cross* a runway, but can never clear you to enter a runway for takeoff purposes. The *why* is also easy—you're asking for an IFR release and a clearance for takeoff. Finally, the *what* is straightforward: the tower controller has to know who you are, where you are, and what you want.

Here is a sample call to the tower when you are ready for takeoff:

CENTENNIAL TOWER, BONANZA THREE–
EIGHT–NINER–KILO–BRAVO IS READY TO GO
RUNWAY THREE–FIVE RIGHT, IFR KANSAS
CITY.

It's not really necessary to repeat that you're IFR and going to Kansas City. However, tower controllers occasionally forget who is going where; therefore, it can't hurt to remind the tower that a release from ATC must be obtained before they let you go.

The tower will typically tell you to hold short while awaiting your IFR release. If the delay gets too long, call back and politely remind the controller you're still awaiting takeoff. Once the release comes from ATC, the tower will clear you onto the runway for takeoff:

BONANZA THREE–EIGHT–NINER–KILO–
BRAVO, TAXI INTO POSITION AND HOLD.

Or:

BONANZA THREE–EIGHT–NINER–KILO–
BRAVO, RUNWAY THREE–FIVE RIGHT,
CLEARED FOR TAKEOFF.

NOTE: As with all vital flight information, any clearance onto a runway (or to take off) should *always* be repeated to the controller before you roll. Every year lives are lost and aircraft are destroyed in collisions on runways. The worst airline disaster in history occurred in 1977 when two 747s collided on a fog-enveloped runway at Tenerife in the Canary Islands. Pilots have been known to cross the wrong runway, land on taxiways, or taxi into "position and hold" when the tower said to "hold short." It only takes a second to say "Roger, cleared for takeoff, Niner–Kilo–Bravo" before you release the brakes. If, for some reason, you *aren't* really supposed to take off, that readback could save your life.

Takeoff from an Uncontrolled Airport

As noted in chapter 6, when you take off from an uncontrolled airport, you will have received a "release time" and a "void time" with your clearance. You must depart between these two times. Remember, your IFR clearance doesn't take effect until the release time, and it expires automatically after the void time. Once you depart the airport within the time allotted, your flight plan is still not activated until you contact ATC on the departure frequency specified in the clearance.

Calling Departure Control

As you leave the airport area, you become the responsibility of the departure controller. The control tower (if there was one) will instruct you to "contact departure, good day." They won't give you the frequency—you should already have it in your clearance—unless you ask. If you left from a field with no tower, contact departure as soon as you are safely out of the airport's traffic pattern.

Your initial call to departure is fairly simple, but it comes at a busy time. You are setting climb power, watching for traffic (if you're out of clouds), and making turns to follow your clearance. Dialing in a new frequency at this time can be distracting, so it's a good idea to have the departure frequency preset on one of the comm radios if possible. It's moments like this when you really appreciate the "flip-flop" capability of many digitally tuned radios.

Departure Control: WHO, WHY, and WHAT

For this first call to departure, think about: (1) *whom* you're calling—the departure controller, who is in charge of your flight as you transition from takeoff, through the initial climb, until you leave the vicinity; (2) *why* you're calling—to let the controller know you are off the ground as planned and to verify that your transponder is working; and (3) *what* they want to know—who you are, where you took off from, and your altitude.

Departure Control: Sample Radio Call

This is an appropriate first call to Departure Control after a handoff (or when you first enter controlled airspace):

> DENVER DEPARTURE, BONANZA THREE–EIGHT–NINER–KILO–BRAVO WITH YOU, OFF FROM CENTENNIAL, CLIMBING THROUGH SIX THOUSAND FOR ONE–THREE THOUSAND.

Notice the use of the phrase "with you" in the above example. As discussed in chapter 3, saying "with you" alerts a facility that your flight information should be on one of the data strips in front of the controller. Every controller or facility you contact should be expecting you whenever a handoff takes place. If they aren't expecting you, saying "with you" tells them that they ought to be. This phrase is usually used in the first radio call after each handoff or frequency change.

The Transition to En Route Flight

As you clear the local traffic area, the departure controller may vector you around other traffic or instruct you to climb to a higher altitude. When you approach cruise altitude, join the flight-planned route, and/or depart the service area of this controller, you move into the next phase of IFR flight—the en route phase.

PART THREE

En Route Communications

CHAPTER 8

From One Controller to the Next: The Handoff

Every IFR flight includes handoffs. The handoff is the process by which control of (and responsibility for) your flight is "handed off" from one controller to another. When you fly to the boundary of a controller's service area, you're handed off to the neighboring sector (or to the next facility). If you take off from a controlled airport, the tower hands you off to the departure controller once you clear the area. Approach controllers hand you off to the arrival tower. Wherever you fly, when you go IFR you will be handed off at least a few times.

Handoffs are not the same as "suggested" or "approved" frequency changes for VFR flight. If you depart VFR from a controlled field, the local tower will approve a change of frequency as soon as you leave the airport traffic pattern. This approval is not a handoff—the tower controller is merely saying, "You are clear of my area, so I don't have to talk to you anymore right now. You are therefore free to change to another frequency or even turn your radio off. It's up to you."

In contrast, a handoff is an instruction from a controller with which you must comply as soon as practicable. The things that distinguish handoffs are: (1) a "flight strip" containing information about you and your flight plan, transmitted to every ATC facility along your route (see chapter 4); and (2) direct contact (usually by telephone) between the two controllers involved.

As you near the limit of one controller's service area, that controller contacts the next controller in line to handle your flight. This one may cover a sector adjacent to yours (and thus may be sitting in the same room as the first controller), or might be located hundreds of miles away in the next ARTCC. The first controller advises the other that your flight is approaching the other's service area, and asks if the receiving controller can take over the flight. The receiving controller should have a flight strip for your flight, so there is no need for controllers to pass along all the details of your flight, such as type of aircraft, souls on board, route of flight, and so forth.

The receiving controller must identify your aircraft on radar (or otherwise accept your flight) before the first controller can hand you off. Once the second controller accepts the flight, you will receive a call telling you to contact (facility name) on (frequency). The transmission frequently ends with "Good day." While this is primarily a gesture of courtesy, it's also a subtle way of saying to the pilot, "That's all I have to say to you. You should acknowledge the call I just made, but don't expect to hear from me again."

Out with the Old Controller, In with the New

The first controller's handoff call to you was merely an instruction to contact a new controller and to use a new frequency. If the name of the "new" facility is the same as the facility you're presently talking to, you know that you're being handed off between sectors at one Center. If you're traveling beyond the reach of one facility, you'll be told to call a new Center (or "approach," or perhaps a tower). The handoff instructions should sound something like this:

CHEROKEE THREE–EIGHT–NINER–KILO–
BRAVO, CONTACT ATLANTA CENTER NOW,
ONE–TWO–FOUR–POINT–SEVEN–FIVE, GOOD
DAY.

As with all important information, you should jot down the new frequency as the controller reads it to you. Draw a single line through the old frequency on your note pad (you have been keeping a list of frequencies, haven't you?). Don't scratch out the frequency completely, as you'll have to call back on the old frequency if there's no answer on the new one.

Next, you reply to the instruction. An appropriate reply combines an acknowledgment of the instruction with a readback of the frequency:

NINER–KILO–BRAVO, ROGER, ONE–TWO–
FOUR–POINT–SEVEN–FIVE, GOOD DAY.

At this point, you and this controller are finished talking to one another (unless you read back the wrong frequency—and you'll hear about it if you do). It's now time to switch from the old frequency to the new and see if anyone out there in this new sector is listening.

After you tune to the new frequency, wait a few seconds before calling. You have to allow your radio time to lock onto the frequency and then you should listen for other radio traffic. If there's no one else speaking at the moment, go ahead and contact the new controller.

The Handoff: WHO, WHY, and WHAT

You already know *whom* you're calling—the next en route controller in charge of your flight. *Why* you're calling is also obvious—the last controller instructed you to call. You are merely trying to establish contact so that the new controller will know you're there on the frequency. The *what*-to-say list is short: Give your aircraft ID; position, if required (see chapter 9); and altitude. If you're climbing or descending, tell the controller your *present* altitude as well as the altitude to which you have been cleared. Finally, if you're proceeding on an assigned vector, say so.

The Handoff: Sample Radio Calls

1. When in radar contact (no position report required):

ATLANTA CENTER, CHEROKEE THREE–
EIGHT–NINER–KILO–BRAVO WITH YOU,
LEVEL AT ONE–ZERO THOUSAND.

2. When a position report is required (chapter 9 explains proper position reporting):

ATLANTA CENTER, CHEROKEE THREE–
EIGHT–NINER–KILO–BRAVO WITH YOU, LEV-
EL AT ONE–ZERO THOUSAND [position report].

3. When climbing or descending:

ATLANTA CENTER, CHEROKEE THREE–
EIGHT–NINER–KILO–BRAVO WITH YOU,
CLIMBING OUT OF FOUR THOUSAND SEVEN
HUNDRED FOR ONE–ZERO THOUSAND.

4. When flying an assigned vector:

ATLANTA CENTER, CHEROKEE THREE–
EIGHT–NINER–KILO–BRAVO WITH YOU AT
ONE–ZERO THOUSAND, HEADING THREE–
ONE–ZERO, VECTORS FOR TRAFFIC.

What to Expect in Reply

After your initial contact, the controller will respond with
your aircraft ID, the statement "radar contact" (if applicable), and the altimeter setting nearest you (if you're flying below 18,000 feet):

NOVEMBER THREE–EIGHT–NINER–KILO–
BRAVO, ROGER, RADAR CONTACT. KNOX-
VILLE ALTIMETER THREE–ZERO–ZERO–FOUR.

Inquiring Controllers Want to Know

Until you reach the end of this new controller's service
area, you will communicate with the same person (usually)
on the same frequency. Sometimes another controller will
relieve the first one, or you will get a new frequency on
which to call the *same* person. Whatever you and this controller talk about, your radio calls need not be so formal
and programmed as the initial handoff. You can use the
abbreviated call sign for your aircraft. If you're asked a
question, you simply answer it. If you want to request a
new altitude or route, call and advise the controller that

you have a request. When time permits, the ATC will ask you what they can do for you and will usually comply if they can.

You must also contact ATC with the following reports, even if you aren't asked. The FARs and the *AIM* require you to report:

- when you leave any previously assigned altitude for a newly-assigned altitude;
- when you change altitudes, if you are operating under a "VFR on Top" clearance;
- when you are unable to maintain a climb/descent rate of at least 500 feet per minute;
- when you execute a missed approach (always accompany this report with a statement of your intentions; e.g., a request to hold, fly another approach, or proceed to your alternate airport);
- when your average *true* airspeed (at cruise) varies by more than five percent (or 10 knots, whichever is greater) from the true airspeed filed in your flight plan;
- when you reach a holding fix or your clearance limit (tell ATC the name of the fix, the time you arrived, and your altitude);
- when you leave any assigned point or holding fix;
- any loss or impairment of navigational or air-to-ground communications ability, including loss of VOR, TACAN, DME, ADF, low frequency navigation receiver, or ILS receiver capability; and
- any information "relating to the safety of flight." If you think this sounds vague, you're right. In deciding whether to report a specific item, a good guideline is to ask yourself, "If I were the controller, would I *want* to

know about this?" If so, tell ATC; if it turns out they don't need to know, there's no harm done.

In addition to the above nine reports, ATC also requires you to report the following if your aircraft is *not* in radar contact (again, even if you aren't asked):

- when you leave the final approach fix (inbound on final approach) on a non-precision approach, or leave the outer marker (or other fix used in place of an outer marker) on a precision approach; or
- when you find that your actual arrival time at any fix will vary from your earlier estimated arrival time by more than three minutes.

If Problems Arise

Sometimes you get no response on a new frequency after a handoff. If you make a call and hear no response, try again once or twice. If the frequency is silent (or, at least, no one answers *you*) for a full minute, something may be amiss.

Many factors can prevent effective two-way communications. The most common culprit in loss of transmit-receive ability is distance. When you change frequencies for a handoff, the two adjoining antenna sites can be quite remote from each other. Sometimes the new site is beyond the effective range of your radio equipment. Perhaps you receive the new facility, but they don't hear you. On the other hand, they may hear you clearly, but you don't hear their replies. Other causes of nonresponse include heavy controller workload (they heard you but forgot about you), or low cruise altitude (terrain is blocking your radio signals).

Regardless of the circumstances, your actions should be the same. When you get no response on a new frequency, always verify that: (1) the radio is correctly tuned to the new frequency; (2) the push-to-talk button is not stuck in the open position; and (3) the volume and squelch are still properly set. Once you have determined that you're using the radio correctly, retune it to the frequency you were using before the handoff (you still have that frequency written down, right?), and call the previous controller. After you establish contact, explain that you have been unable to make contact on the new frequency.

When making this call, be sure to state what frequency you've been trying to use. The reason for this is simple: It's easy to copy the wrong frequency during a handoff. When you were told to change frequency, your readback may have been incorrect without the controller noticing (or perhaps you didn't read back the new frequency at all). In either case, you may have been calling someone who wasn't there. Telling the controller what frequency you've been trying to use allows for a recheck of your readback:

MEMPHIS CENTER, CHEROKEE THREE–EIGHT–NINER–KILO–BRAVO IS BACK WITH YOU, NEGATIVE CONTACT ON ONE–TWO–FOUR–POINT–SEVEN–FIVE.

This means, "I'm back on the frequency with you again. I couldn't make contact on the new frequency I copied down, 124.75. Please advise."

ATC will acknowledge your situation, and perhaps offer an explanation for the problem. If 124.75 MHz is not the right frequency, for example, the controller will tell you (again) that you should call on 124.55, not 75. If, on the other hand, 124.75 is correct, ATC will attempt to resolve the difficulty. One controller usually contacts the other via telephone to find out whether your earlier calls on the new frequency were heard at all. This helps the first controller determine whether there is a problem with ATC's reception/transmission, or yours, or both.

Whatever the trouble, ATC will require you to remain in radio contact until you can be safely handed off to the next controller. Unlike VFR flight following, the controllers don't have the option of telling you to squawk 1200 and "try Center again in about twenty miles." They must maintain contact with you. Your job, therefore, in case of a snag during a handoff, is to keep ATC advised of your status and let them tell you what to do.

CHAPTER 9

Reporting Your Position

Knowing where you are is crucial to ATC. In order to control traffic safely and effectively, controllers balance the need for adequate separation between aircraft with the need to expedite the flow of traffic in and around congested areas. In the absence of radar service, reporting your position to ATC is what makes the controller's job possible.

In chapter 4, we observed that today's IFR environment is mostly radar-equipped; that is, unless you fly in the more remote areas of the nation, most of your IFR flights will be conducted while in radar contact. ATC is watching you and knows where you are at all times. In addition to keeping track of your progress, a controller watching a radar display can provide traffic advisories when needed and (sometimes) limited weather information.

When you do find yourself straying beyond the limits of radar coverage, however, safe IFR flight is still feasible.

The only difference is that you are charged with keeping ATC informed of your progress. This is managed with *position reports* made at regular intervals, as specified by the charts (or by controllers).

Position reporting is well-known to most high-time instrument pilots; in fact, widespread radar service is relatively new. Until the last two decades, radar coverage was mostly allocated to high-traffic areas or military installations. All those operating IFR between radar-equipped locations were expected to report their aircraft's position and altitude regularly. The controllers at nonradar facilities kept track of aircraft by moving small wedge-shaped markers around (by hand) on large tabletop maps of the area. These markers, nicknamed "shrimp boats," are still available as a worst-case backup system at ATC facilities.

Although there are lots of reasons why radar service is limited in certain areas, three key factors predominate. First, some regions are simply not equipped with complete radar coverage. Second, many radar installations are surrounded by high terrain, which obstructs low-angle radar signals; thus, coverage is only available for aircraft at higher altitudes, even though the MEA is comparatively low. Finally, electrical or mechanical equipment failures can temporarily disable radar service in a particular sector (or an entire facility).

When Are Position Reports Needed?

Anytime ATC cannot see your aircraft on radar, you must make regular position reports. On most IFR flights, when you check in with the departure or en route controller, your initial call is acknowledged with the phrase, "Radar contact." This statement, though not repeated during subsequent handoffs, remains valid until you hear otherwise.

Once any controller confirms you are on radar, therefore, you assume each succeeding controller still has you on the screen.

If a controller later says, "Radar contact lost," or "Radar service terminated," you are to resume position reporting until radar contact is reestablished. Of course, if ATC never has you in radar contact to begin with, you must make position reports throughout the entire flight.

Reporting Points: Where to Find Them

In order to keep track of all aircraft in a given area, ATC designates certain fixes as "reporting points." These points are either compulsory reporting points or "on request" (at the controller's option) reporting points. When you're not in radar contact, you *must* report reaching any compulsory reporting point. These are the points marked as solid triangles on the en route charts. You only report reaching an on-request reporting point if ATC asks you to do so. These optional points are marked as open triangles on the en route charts.

Reporting Points: When Do You Get There?

The *AIM* specifies the precise moment when you "reach" a reporting point. It's important to note the exact time of passage, because position reports should be accurate to the minute (see p. 99). The way you record your arrival time is dependent upon the type of fix or identifier you are using:

- When you're told to report passing a VOR or VOR-TAC, report the time at which the to/from indicator first reverses itself completely.

- When the reporting point is a nondirectional beacon (NDB) or compass locator, report the time when the indicator makes its first complete reversal.
- When marking station passage with an audible or marker-light warning (e.g., when passing a fan marker or Z marker), note the time the signal is first received and the time it stops—the average of these two times is the reported time of passage.

Position Reports: Sample Radio Calls

According to the FAA, the following information must be included in an IFR position report:

(a) Aircraft identification

(b) Position (name of fix or identifier)

(c) Time you reached that position (minutes past the hour)

(d) Altitude or flight level

(e) Name of the next reporting point on your route and your estimated time of arrival (ETA) at that point

(f) Name of the next succeeding reporting point and

(g) Any "pertinent remarks"

Here is a sample position report for an aircraft over the St. Louis VORTAC while you are en route to Springfield via the Vichy VORTAC. You noted a complete reversal of the to/from indicator over St. Louis at 3:25 P.M. local time (2025 Zulu, or "two–five" past the hour), and you expect to arrive at Vichy (72 nm away) in twenty-six minutes (which will be 2051, or "five–one" past the hour):

KANSAS CITY CENTER, BARON THREE–EIGHT–NINER–KILO–BRAVO OVER SAINT LOUIS AT

TWO–FIVE, LEVEL AT SEVEN THOUSAND. EX-PECT VICHY AT FIVE–ONE, THEN SPRINGFIELD.

ATC's response will be an acknowledgment of the report, and any information you may need (such as the local altimeter setting or a revised clearance).

After making a position report, you may be asked to report reaching some additional fix if the controller needs an update on your position more frequently. The above position report, for example, tells ATC that you will next report upon reaching Vichy and that the controller should not expect to hear from you until fifty-one minutes past the hour (twenty-six minutes from now). But if heavy traffic (and a lack of radar coverage) along that route has the controller concerned about aircraft spacing, you may be asked to report some intermediate point, such as the Foristell VORTAC:

BARON NINER–KILO–BRAVO, ROGER. REPORT REACHING FORISTELL VORTAC.

If a controller tells you to report reaching such an on-request reporting point, be sure to write down the name of that reporting point, then acknowledge the instructions:

CENTER, NINER–KILO–BRAVO, ROGER. WILL REPORT FORISTELL.

Take this time to locate your new reporting fix on the map. If it's an intersection, you may need to adjust the radials set into your nav heads or change frequencies.

Changing the ETA

Remember, from chapter 7, that if you aren't in radar contact you must inform ATC if a prior ETA at any reporting point will vary by more than three minutes. Assume, for instance, that in the above example you encounter a 20-knot headwind (which always seems to happen anyway) between St. Louis and Vichy. After a few quick entries on the flight computer, your new ETA at Vichy turns out to be 2055 (thirty minutes from St. Louis, and four minutes later than originally reported). In this situation, you must call ATC as soon as this information becomes available.

KANSAS CITY CENTER, BARON THREE–
EIGHT–NINER–KILO–BRAVO, REVISED ETA
FOR VICHY IS FIVE–FIVE (DUE TO HEAD-
WIND).

The comment about the headwind is optional, but it serves two purposes: it explains the revised ETA, and it gives the controller some idea of the current wind conditions in that area at your altitude.

In Conclusion

Position reporting is just another stepping-stone along the IFR trail. Like every radio call, the position report is easy to master. You don't have to memorize the list of elements in a good position report in order to give one correctly. As with all IFR communications, the best procedure is to think about whom you're calling and why, and then ask yourself, "What will this person want to know?" The name "position report" says it all: Just tell the controller where you are, at what time, and when you'll be at the next fix. With a little experience, you'll find the details will fill themselves in.

CHAPTER 10

Revised Clearances

When ATC Changes Its Mind

On rare occasions, your IFR flight will follow the route in the original clearance. From the time you contact departure until you are cleared to land, the only thing controllers will tell you is whom to call on a handoff and at what altitudes to fly. On arrival at the destination, your note pad is curiously free from erasures and stray marks. It's almost as if you were the only one flying that day.

The other ninety-nine percent of the time, however, your clearance will be revised at least a few times. Remember that the original clearance often includes special departure procedures to keep you clear of expected traffic in the area. If that traffic doesn't materialize or if it clears out sooner than expected, ATC may clear you back onto your flight-planned route before you've completed all the original departure procedures. If, on the other hand, forecast traffic or weather conditions along your route worsen, you may be forced to deviate onto a longer route than you prefer. This happens most often when flying toward large, crowded terminal areas.

Regardless of the reason, however, these occasional revisions in ATC's instructions are "revised clearances." A revised clearance is important because it modifies, *for the rest of the flight,* any component of the clearance it affects. For example, if you receive a new altitude, you fly that altitude until otherwise instructed, even if your first clearance contained a completely different one. The original clearance may have included turns, vectors, and holds just to get to a VOR, but if it is later revised and you are told to go *direct* to that VOR, the earlier instructions are void. You just go to the VOR.

Sample Revisions to a Clearance

Let's look at the sample route of flight from chapter 6 and the clearance that goes with it. In the example, the original route of flight you filed from Dallas/Fort Worth to Little Rock is:

DALLAS/FORT WORTH DFW—DIRECT BUJ—V66 SLR—V66 TXK—V54 LIT—ADAMS LIT.

Translated, the requested route is: "From Dallas/Fort Worth Airport, direct to the Blue Ridge VORTAC, Victor 66 to the Sulphur Springs and Texarkana VORTACs, Victor 54 to the Little Rock VORTAC, then to Adams Field in Little Rock."

After processing your requested route, the FAA gave you this route clearance:

DFW—HEADING 030 VECTORS KMART—AS FILED.

This translates to: "From DFW Regional Airport, after departure turn right to heading 030° for radar vectors to

KMART intersection, then cleared as filed" (Blue Ridge, Victor Airways 66 and 54 to Little Rock).

So far, so good. The only deviation from the route you originally filed is a vector to KMART, but since that's fairly close to Blue Ridge anyway, it shouldn't cost you too much time or fuel.

Now suppose you departed Runway 35 Right at DFW, made a right turn to 030° at a safe altitude, and called Departure when instructed to do so. Departure acknowledge radar contact, and clears you to 3,000 feet (the original altitude in the chapter 6 clearance was only 2,000). You've just received a revised clearance—a new altitude. From now until ATC clears you to another altitude, 3,000 is where you should stay.

After a few minutes, however, ATC calls again and says:

CENTURION NINER–KILO–BRAVO, CLIMB AND MAINTAIN NINER THOUSAND. FLY HEADING ZERO–FOUR–ZERO, UPON RECEIVING BLUE RIDGE PROCEED DIRECT BLUE RIDGE, THEN AS FILED.

This is another revised clearance, albeit a little more complex than the last one. First, it's another altitude clearance. You were level at 3,000 feet, but now must climb (at 500 feet per minute or faster) to 9,000 feet. At long last, ATC gave you the altitude they told you to expect in the original clearance ("Expect Niner Thousand . . ."). But that's not all this clearance is—it's also a new *route* clearance. Instead of proceeding to KMART intersection ("Darn! I had my nav radios all set up for it!"), you turn right to 040° and proceed direct to the Blue Ridge VOR-TAC as soon as you receive a reliable signal.

So what happened to your clearance to KMART? It's now void, expired, superseded, moot, irrelevant, terminated, lapsed, invalid (feel free to insert your favorite synonyms), and otherwise no longer in effect. Your clearance has been *revised*, and so the old route is replaced with the new.

What About Communications?

There are two rules to remember when you receive a revised clearance, whether the revision is simple ("Turn right ten degrees") or complex (an entirely new route, complete with holding instructions): (1) Write everything down; and (2) read back all the important information.

You already know the importance of writing down every instruction. Your memory may be good, but it's not as accurate as a written record. If you are keeping a laptop communications log (see chapter 2), writing down new instructions is easy. When you get a new altitude, cross out the one at the bottom of the "altitudes" list and then add the new one. Do likewise for new frequencies. If you receive a new routing or vector, write it down in "clearance shorthand" near the first. Cross out those parts of the old clearance that have been replaced (e.g., the KMART instructions and altitudes on the original sample clearance).

Now that you have the instructions jotted down (the entire procedure should only take a few seconds), repeat them to ATC. As you know, a readback helps you and ATC guard against a misstated (or misunderstood) clearance. The following readback tells the departure controller that you have all the information you need, and that you have it copied down correctly:

NINER–KILO–BRAVO, ROGER, ZERO–FOUR–ZERO, DIRECT BLUE RIDGE WHEN ABLE, OUT OF THREE THOUSAND FOR NINER THOUSAND.

If you're thinking there's no real trick to this "readback" business, you're right. A proper readback is one that tells ATC you understood their instructions and will comply with them. Key items such as fix names, altitudes, headings, and other "safety of flight" instructions should be repeated. If you're ever in doubt about whether to repeat something, it's best to err on the conservative side and read it back. As you practice a little, your readbacks will get shorter (but remain complete)—yet another trademark of a skilled IFR communicator.

In Conclusion

The IFR environment is dynamic. Controller workloads, traffic, and weather change continually. A safe IFR pilot is always prepared for change and adapts easily as conditions dictate. A revised clearance—whether a new vector or a whole new route—is just one minor variable that you must expect and deal with.

CHAPTER 11

Going Off the ATC Frequency

When You Have Other Things to Do

There are many reasons to "go off frequency," that is, contact someone other than ATC during an IFR flight. Unforecast winds or weather along your route may prompt you to call Flight Watch for updated weather information. An encounter with turbulence, icing, or wind shear is good reason to call in a pilot report, or PIREP. As you approach your destination, you should listen to the ATIS information in the area. Sometimes you just want to call the destination FBO to arrange services or to report your ETA. No matter what the reason, however, contacting someone else means first breaking radio contact with ATC. But since communication between aircraft and ATC is the glue that binds the IFR system, going off frequency should be done only for a good reason and for brief periods.

Before You Go

If you want to avoid talking to others when you fly, wait for a clear day and go VFR. When you fly IFR, you may not break radio contact with ATC without permission (except in an emergency). Pilots are required to maintain contact throughout IFR flights because ATC can't control traffic without voice communication. Traffic conditions permitting, however, ATC will usually authorize a brief frequency change if the pilot requests it. But if too many aircraft break contact at once, the air traffic controller is no longer a controller but an observer. If this happens, the IFR system breaks down and the results could be disastrous. If you decide go off frequency, then, make certain that (*a*) it's really necessary, (*b*) you get the go-ahead from ATC before switching, and (*c*) you don't take too long.

Frequency Change Approved

To get permission from ATC to change frequencies, you must inform the controller handling your flight that you have a request. As in most situations where you want a favor, timing is important. Wait until a slow time in the flight to make your request. If the controller is busy with twelve or fifteen aircraft in a busy area, and you're due to be handed off (or cleared for the approach to your destination) in two minutes, it's probably not a good time to break contact with ATC. If, on the other hand, you're at cruise altitude with plenty of time remaining in the flight, and you hear only occasional radio traffic on the frequency, chances are the controller can afford to lose you for a few minutes.

The first radio call to ATC is very simple—just tell the controller you have a request:

CENTER, LEARJET NINER–KILO–BRAVO, RE-QUEST.

This short call is extremely useful in getting a controller's attention without congesting the frequency. Use it any time you want assistance but are not in a hurry. Note also the abbreviated term "Center" and the shortened call sign for your aircraft. As mentioned earlier, it's only appropriate to use these brief identifiers *after* you've established contact with a given controller.

Once you let ATC know you need something, Center may ask you to stand by for a while, but will eventually tell you to "go ahead with your request." Explain that you need to contact another facility, and why:

CENTER, NINER–KILO–BRAVO, REQUEST PERMISSION TO GO OFF FREQUENCY TO OBTAIN WEATHER ADVISORY.

If your absence from the frequency will not pose a problem, you should hear:

NINER–KILO–BRAVO, ROGER. FREQUENCY CHANGE APPROVED. RETURN TO THIS FREQUENCY WITHIN THREE MINUTES; ADVISE UPON RETURNING.

The controller's response may include a time restriction (as in this example) or other instructions. As always, acknowledge the instructions and adhere to them. If you can't return within three minutes, then don't change frequencies at all. The safety of your flight and other aircraft in the area depend upon your contact with ATC.

One final suggestion: If you have two comm radios in your aircraft (and if not, you should), monitor ATC on one radio while you switch frequencies and call the other ground facility on the second. If you use a headset, switch the ATC radio to "speaker" and set the volume so that you can hear it in the background. If you only use the speaker when you fly, turn the ATC radio down—but not so far that you can't hear it—during your time on the new frequency. "Monitoring" the ATC frequency in this way provides a nice benefit: You can talk to the other facility and listen for ATC radio traffic at the same time. Also, you provide yourself with an extra safety margin in case things get busy with ATC while you're still waiting for confirmation on your rental car. Being out of touch with ATC is like leaving your aircraft on autopilot while you read a book; it might work all right most of the time, but it's not a good situation to be in if anything goes wrong. Monitoring ATC, therefore, decreases the chance of trouble if the controller needs you back on the frequency. If you hear serious traffic conflicts, sudden weather problems, or some emergency reported on the ATC channel, you can cut short the conversation with the FBO or Flight Watch and reestablish contact with your controller.

Weather Information: En Route Flight Advisory Service

The *Airman's Information Manual* defines En Route Flight Advisory Service (EFAS) as "a service specifically designed to provide en route aircraft with timely and meaningful weather advisories pertinent to the type of flight intended, route of flight, and altitude." EFAS is also the major facility for collecting and distributing Pilot Reports (see p. 113).

Complete, timely weather information is vital for safe IFR operations, yet the weather is in a constant state of flux—it changes minute by minute, hour by hour. The forecast you receive with your initial flight briefing is rarely identical to the weather you really find at altitude. EFAS, therefore, is a valuable resource for updating the weather information affecting your flight as the weather changes.

EFAS is provided by specially trained Flight Service Station personnel located in select FSSs around the country. It is identified by the call sign "Flight Watch," and uses the frequency 122.0 MHz. Through remote communications outlets (RCOs) covering large areas, EFAS is normally available everywhere in the coterminous United States (and Puerto Rico) for aircraft flying at 5,000 feet a.g.l. or higher.* Flight Watch specialists are usually on duty from 6:00 A.M. to 10:00 P.M. local time†

According to the *AIM,* Flight Watch is not the proper facility to call when you wish to file or close a flight plan, report your position, obtain a preflight briefing, or get random weather reports or forecasts. Instead, EFAS provides current conditions and updated forecasts *along your route* and collects information regarding storms, icing, winds, and turbulence from aircraft in flight.

To contact Flight Watch, tune to 122.0 and call the nearest EFAS control station (by name, if you know it; check the *Airport Facilities Directory*) and name the VOR or VORTAC nearest your position:

NASHVILLE FLIGHT WATCH, LEARJET THREE–EIGHT–NINER–KILO–BRAVO, NEAR GRAHAM VORTAC.

---

* Note that this altitude is 5,000 feet *above ground level.* Over mountainous terrain, therefore, you may be unable to contact Flight Watch when flying below 10,000–20,000 feet msl.

† "Local time" refers to the time at the control station itself, not necessarily the remote outlet you're communicating through. As a result, the availability times for EFAS services may vary plus or minus one hour for remote outlets near time-zone boundaries.

Stating your approximate position tells the Flight Watch specialist which remote outlet to use in answering your call. If you don't have the name of the nearest EFAS station handy, you can make the above call without using a name—the appropriate station will hear and answer with its identifier.

Flight Watch: WHO, WHY, and WHAT

After you establish contact with Flight Watch, then what? Hopefully, you had a specific purpose in mind before you left the ATC frequency. If you didn't call just to make a pilot report, you must request any weather information you want. Appropriate requests include an updated weather or winds-aloft forecast along your route, current conditions at your destination, or reports on any significant weather activity in your area.

What service you want determines what you should say after the specialist responds to your call. Flight Watch frequencies are usually less congested than ATC frequencies, so you can afford to be a bit more "conversational" with your request. All you have to do is explain where you are (generally), where you're going, and what information you require:

> NINER–KILO–BRAVO IS SOUTHEAST OF THE GRAHAM VORTAC, EN ROUTE TO ATLANTA AT FLIGHT LEVEL THREE–ONE–ZERO. REQUEST CURRENT CONDITIONS AT CHATTANOOGA AND ATLANTA, AND ANY PILOT REPORTS ALONG MY ROUTE.

Of course, you should be ready to copy the information requested, so have your note pad handy. At the conclusion of the reports, you will almost certainly be asked for a Pilot Report giving current conditions where you are. Even if you haven't encountered any noteworthy weather, Flight Watch still wants to know. As the *AIM* says:

> Pilot participation is essential to the success of EFAS through a continuous exchange of information on winds, turbulence, visibility, icing, etc., between pilots in flight and Flight Watch specialists on the ground. Pilots are encouraged to report *good as well as bad* and *expected as well as unexpected* flight conditions to Flight Watch facilities.

The Significance of Pilot Reports

As an observer sitting in your aircraft at altitude, you are uniquely able to report to others precise weather conditions along your route. The PIREP is the vehicle through which you inform the FAA of weather you encounter. The accuracy of a PIREP greatly exceeds that of a National Weather Service (NWS) forecast, because the PIREP is a "right now" report from the air, rather than a "this is what we think it might be" prediction made by observers on the ground.

PIREPs are put to use by many different agencies and facilities. Your local TRACON uses them to expedite the flow of air traffic in the area and to help aircraft avoid hazardous weather during departure or arrival. The FSS includes PIREPs in preflight or en route weather briefings to pilots who request them. Center uses the reports to determine the best altitudes for en route traffic and to issue hazardous weather advisories. PIREPs allow the NWS to verify, update, or amend current forecasts or advisories. Sometimes, in fact, it is a PIREP that triggers an area-wide advisory for hazardous weather. Finally, the NWS, the military, and other government and private industry groups use PIREPs for meteorological research.

Pilot Reports: Whom and When to Call

Although Flight Watch is the primary collection point for PIREPs, all FAA ground facilities are required to solicit them when conditions warrant. When low ceilings, low visibility, thunderstorms, icing, wind shear, or turbulence are reported or forecast, the ATC facility in that area (whether an FSS, ARTCC, TRACON, or EFAS) may ask for reports from pilots in the vicinity. If you encounter any such weather conditions, but don't wish to go off frequency to tell Flight Watch, simply report it to the controller handling your flight. The information will still make its way to the FSS network.

Pilot Reports are not just useful for monitoring severe weather, however. Because the PIREP offers a special "on-the-spot" description of current weather conditions, the FAA urges pilots to report almost any atmospheric data available. If time allows during the en route phase of your flight, therefore, call Flight Watch and tell them about: (1) cloud bases, tops, and layers; (2) flight visibility; (3) precipitation; (4) visibility restrictions (e.g., haze, smoke, or dust); (5) winds aloft; or (6) air temperatures at altitude.

Pilot Reports: What to Include

There are thirteen possible elements to a PIREP broadcast by the FAA, though not all elements are present in every report. The first six are included in every transmitted PIREP, and one or more of items 7 through 13 are present when required. Your report to the ground facility need not include all these elements, of course, so long as you supply all information relevant to the weather you're reporting. After you supply the available weather information, the ground facility compiles and issues the report in this format:

1. *Station identifier*: The three-letter identifier for the weather-reporting location nearest the weather being reported. This is usually the nearest major airport or FSS, and is supplied by the ground facility that takes the report.
2. *Report type*: PIREPs are classified as "routine" or "urgent." The ground facility will determine the classification based on the information received.
3. *Location of observation*: The location of the weather observed. You should report this location as an approximate radial-and-distance from a VOR or VORTAC.
4. *Time*: Time of report in Zulu time.
5. *Altitude*: Altitude, or flight level, where the phenomenon is observed. While always important, this item is essential for turbulence and icing reports.
6. *Type of aircraft*: This is also essential for icing or turbulence reports, because ice accumulation or turbulent air means different things to large and small aircraft. Chop considered "moderate" by the pilot of a Boeing 767 might take the wings off a Skyhawk; icing that a Baron pilot reports as "severe" might only amount to a trace of ice on a corporate jet.

7. *Sky cover*: Cloud bases, tops, or layers, as well as overall coverage (scattered, broken, or overcast).

8. *Weather*: Flight visibility, precipitation observed, restrictions to visibility, etc.

9. *Temperature*: Outside air temperature at your altitude. Report this value in degrees Celsius ($C°$). Always include temperature with icing reports.

10. *Winds aloft*: If you've had time to figure wind direction (in degrees magnetic) and speed (in knots) during cruise, report this information as well. E-6Bs, electronic flight computers, some Loran-C units, and most sophisticated VLF or inertial navigation systems allow accurate calculation of these values.

11. *Turbulence*: Report the intensity (light, moderate, severe, or extreme), frequency (occasional, intermittent, or continuous), and duration of any turbulence. Differentiate between "chop" (rhythmic bumpiness) and simple turbulence (momentary, erratic disturbances), when applicable. Also state whether the aircraft was in or near clouds when turbulence was encountered. Consult the *AIM* or a book on aviation weather for more information on the different types of turbulence.

12. *Icing*: Report the intensity (trace, light, moderate, severe), type (rime, clear, or mixed), the outside air temperature ($C°$), and whether the icing was encountered in clouds or in falling precipitation. As with turbulence, you should consult the *AIM* or an aviation weather text for details on icing types and severity.

13. *Remarks*: Any comments or information needed, such as additional weather not mentioned above or clarification of any previously reported items.

Pilot Reports: What to Say

PIREPs are detailed reports, and a complete one includes a lot of information. It's not necessary, however, for you to follow a strict format or use specific phraseology when making a PIREP. "The important thing," says the *AIM*, "is that the information is relayed so other pilots may benefit from your observation." If your initial report is incomplete or needs clarification, the ground facility taking the report will ask for additional information. Still, you should plan PIREPs carefully so that you give a complete report without tying up the frequency.

If you encounter serious, unexpected conditions that need reporting *right now* for the safety of other aircraft, ATC will copy a PIREP directly from you on the Center frequency. PIREPs can take a long time to copy, however, and this may tie up the Center frequency. Whenever your work load (and the controller's) permits, switch to the Flight Watch frequency to make your report. Make contact as detailed above, then inform them you want to make a pilot report:

> FLIGHT WATCH, NINER–KILO–BRAVO HAS
> A PILOT REPORT.

This alerts the station to prepare to copy the report. You'll be given the go-ahead as soon as the specialist is ready to copy. When you transmit the report, give as much information as possible in the first radio call. At a minimum, give the specialist basic elements such as your location, the time of the event, your altitude and type of aircraft, and the significant conditions you're reporting (icing, turbulence, etc.):

> NINER–KILO–BRAVO IS OVER SANTA FE AT
> 1730 ZULU, OCCASIONAL MODERATE TURBU-

LENCE IN CLOUDS AT FLIGHT LEVEL THREE–ONE–ZERO.

Or:

NINER–KILO–BRAVO ENCOUNTERED LIGHT TO MODERATE RIME ICING DURING CLIMB FROM ALBUQUERQUE TO SANTA FE VORTAC AT 1655 ZULU, FROM ONE–ONE THOUSAND TO ONE–FOUR THOUSAND; CLEAR OF CLOUDS NOW AT FLIGHT LEVEL THREE–ONE–ZERO, TEMPERATURE MINUS FOUR–ZERO.

The specialist will ask you for any information you don't include, such as winds aloft, cloud tops, or anything else of interest to the controlling station.

Reporting Wind Shear

The technical definition of wind shear includes any sudden change in wind speed or direction. This includes normal wind shifts encountered by aircraft climbing or descending through the higher altitudes into areas of different wind patterns. When such shifts occur at altitude, it's not usually a problem; it's simply a factor which affects ground speed or heading. If wind shear happens on take-off or landing, however, it can be lethal.

Every pilot should understand the insidious nature of wind shear. Wind shear—like its deadly cousin, the microburst—is not the most violent weather phenomenon, but it may be the most treacherous. The reasons for this are many. Unlike thunderstorms or hurricanes, wind shear is invisible to most weather-sensing equipment and so is almost impossible to predict. It is fast-moving and short-lived—so much so that by the time wind shear is reported

in a given area, it may have changed drastically (or disappeared). Wind shear is particularly dangerous to low-
flying aircraft because it can cause a sudden, unrecoverable
loss of airspeed (and lift) in seconds.

There are numerous articles and book chapters on wind
shear and its effects. The subject is beyond the scope of this
work. Because it is so hazardous and so difficult to anticipate, however, you should always warn other pilots by reporting any brush with low-altitude wind shear. Because
wind shear is a "right now" hazard, you should report it to
the first FAA ground facility you come into contact with, as
soon as you are safely away from the threat. Don't take the
time to call Flight Watch if you're already in touch with the
tower. Report it immediately—you could save lives.

There are a few special terms you should use (and some
to avoid) for wind shear PIREPs. As with other PIREPs,
the most important thing in making a report is to give
enough information to allow other aircraft to steer clear of
the area (or to be ready for the airspeed change if they
encounter it). You should be sure to mention your *general
location, altitude,* and the *effect* on your aircraft (loss or gain
of airspeed, loss of altitude, power required to overcome
the shear, etc.) *Do not* use the terms "positive" or "negative" to describe wind shear. These terms were once used
to indicate the effect on lift and airspeed (e.g., "negative
wind shear" indicated a loss of lift). Reports of "negative
wind shear on approach," however, have been interpreted
as "no wind shear was encountered." To avoid confusion,
simply report the actual effect on airspeed:

AUSTIN TOWER, LEARJET THREE–EIGHT–
NINER–KILO–BRAVO ENCOUNTERED WIND
SHEAR ON FINAL APPROACH. LOST TWO–FIVE
KNOTS AT FOUR HUNDRED FEET.

Or:

CENTENNIAL TOWER, LEARJET THREE–
EIGHT–NINER–KILO–BRAVO ENCOUNTERED
ABRUPT WIND SHEAR ON TAKEOFF AT FIVE
THOUSAND EIGHT HUNDRED FEET, RE-
QUIRED MAXIMUM POWER TO MAINTAIN AL-
TITUDE.

Going Off Frequency: Other Reasons to Leave

While weather updates or PIREPs are common reasons to switch frequencies, they're not the only ones. You can call the nearest FSS to file, modify, or cancel another flight plan (a FSS can't help with the flight plan you're currently on, of course; Flight Service loses control of your flight plan once it's activated). You can even call a private ground facility (such as a company dispatcher or an FBO) to report your ETA, request a rental car, or have a message relayed by telephone.

Any time you go off frequency to call someone else, the rules for communication are still the same: Tell people what you want, give them as much information as possible up front, and don't tie up the frequency. Before you transmit, ask yourself *whom* you're calling, *why* you're calling them, and *what* they will need to know from you when you call.

Flight Watch, FSS, and FBO frequencies are typically not as crowded as ATC frequencies, so the need for brevity and strict phraseology is relaxed. Nevertheless, as a skilled IFR communicator you'll want to minimize your time away from the controller's frequency. Finish your reports, questions, reservations, and other business, and get back to the controller as soon as you can. Only when you're back "on line" with ATC are you operating fully and safely within the IFR system.

Reestablishing Contact with ATC

Having completed your off-frequency business, switch back to the last ATC frequency assigned (unless you were instructed otherwise when you first changed frequencies) and report your return to the controller as soon as there's a break in the radio traffic:

CENTER, LEARJET NINER–KILO–BRAVO IS BACK WITH YOU.

The controller will likely acknowledge your call, and may issue a new altimeter setting or other information if necessary.

The rest of the en route phase continues as before. The latter part of en route flight is a good time to mentally prepare yourself for the transition to the arrival phase. As will be explained in chapter 12, the end of the en route phase of flight is your last opportunity to review charts and procedures before getting truly busy with arrival.

Anticipating the Arrival

So Much to Do,
So Little Time

Catching Your Breath While Looking Ahead

From the time you first establish yourself en route, you should start thinking about what is arguably the hardest part of every IFR flight: approach and landing. Experienced instrument pilots rate different segments of each flight as the most demanding or most unpredictable. While it is true that *all* aspects of flight are demanding and unpredictable, some portions are nevertheless more arduous than others. It makes sense, therefore, for the pilot to take advantage of any lull in the action to prepare mentally for the next busy interval. One of the best times to do so is during the en route segment of the flight. Your only navigational concern is staying on the course centerline; you maintain a constant altitude, engine power is properly adjusted, fuel flows and headwinds have been calculated, and conversations with controllers are limited to handoffs and the occasional altimeter setting. This is the ideal opportunity to ready yourself for the instrument approach.

What's So Tough About Approaches?

Pilot activity and stress levels peak several times during a flight, beginning with taxiing to the run-up area, takeoff, and climbout, and culminating when the aircraft rolls out on landing and exits the active runway. Some recent studies indicate that the highest stress period for most pilots (albeit a brief one) is during takeoff. From the time takeoff power is applied until the aircraft is established in a healthy, positive climb, pilots' respiration rates (i.e., how rapidly they breathe), slow dramatically, almost to the point where many pilots seem to be holding their breath during the entire takeoff roll.

Research notwithstanding, however, the most *prolonged* stress period in a "normal" IFR flight (i.e., one without any emergencies or other problems) is the instrument approach to minimums in solid IMC. The approach to minimums is one of the busiest, and probably *the* most potentially hazardous activity of all those in which instrument pilots are drilled during training. Procedures such as instrument takeoffs, unusual attitude recovery, and partial panel work are all important flight skills for a competent instrument pilot, but the instrument approach differs from all other maneuvers (and becomes a truly critical operation) in one important aspect: Approaches are intended to bring you and your aircraft *closer to the ground*. Sure, you operate near the ground on takeoff as well, but the goal during climbout is to increase your altitude as safely and efficiently as possible.

Focusing on the Really Important Part

In one way or another, all elements of flight safety exist to prevent an unscheduled contact with the terrain below. Early in their training, beginning pilots learn that maintaining a healthy reserve of both altitude and airspeed is vital. Of these, only altitude is truly indispensable. A severe, or even total, loss of airspeed (at a high enough altitude) need not result in a mishap—the pilot simply pitches the nose down and trades some of the reserve altitude for airspeed. But a total loss of altitude—regardless of airspeed—means meeting the ground. If you intend the aircraft to land, and you make the round rubber things touch down first, then there's no problem. Any other ground contact, however, is undesirable (and nearly always destructive).

Since pilots thus use their aircraft and their skills to keep as much altitude as possible between themselves and the earth's surface, it follows that the riskiest (and certainly one of the most stressful) aspect of flight is flying near the ground while descending toward it. Since descent and landing are what instrument approaches are all about, anything you can do to organize yourself (and your thoughts) before the approach begins will help provide an added margin of safety.

The arrival phase is also the most communications-intensive segment of flight. Even if you're the only aircraft in the area, Approach Control still has to manage your flight through your descent to the initial approach altitude, vector you to some initial or final approach fix, and hand you off to tower or advisory frequency just as you get really busy keeping the needles centered and configuring for landing. Your final approach clearance will abound with information to copy and assimilate while your hands are full with flying the airplane. It's good policy, then, to spend the last few minutes of en route level flight focusing on the really important part of your flight: the part that brings you down in one piece.

Sorting Out the Paperwork

Communicating means exchanging information. Keeping your inflight communications well organized, then, is only possible when you keep all necessary flight information organized. Assuming you have all the current charts and approach plates with you (you verified all that before you departed, right?), organization means knowing where everything is and having it in sight or within easy reach.

Knowing which approach to expect at your destination isn't tricky. Just check the wind and weather information for the area, and review any NOTAMs you received with your preflight briefing. To get the weather, tune in an ATIS or AWOS (Automated Weather Observation System) from your destination (or some nearby airport, if the destination doesn't have such a service) using your number two comm radio.* If you're too far away to receive the ATIS, or if you only have one comm, go off frequency to get an update from Flight Watch. If it sounds as though the weather at your destination is at or near minimums, be sure to get an update on your alternate as well. Once you

* HINT: If the ATC frequency is fairly busy, and you're worried about missing something while copying the ATIS, try switching the number two comm to the cabin speaker while monitoring ATC on your headset. Slide one earphone off your ear, and you'll be able to hear both frequencies simultaneously. You might be surprised at how easy it is to focus your attention on the ATIS information on the speaker, yet stay aware of what's happening on the ATC frequency at the same time. When you finish, simply replace the headset over both ears and disconnect the number two radio from the speaker.

have the current weather, you can probably guess which is the active runway (based on the wind direction) and what approach to expect.* Move the approach plates for that runway to the top of your stack and look them over in detail.

Analyzing the Approach Procedures

Begin by locating yourself on the en route chart. Just as you learned to do for VFR sectional charts on a cross-country flight, orient the chart on your lap so that your present heading (on the map) points out the front of the airplane. Granted, you can't really use the chart this way for very long (frequencies and identifiers are hard to read upside down), but it gives you the best mental picture of your position relative to your destination, and will help you visualize your entry into the published approach procedure. If the aircraft is equipped with a moving map display, you already know how helpful this kind of picture can be when trying to maintain your orientation in the clouds.

Now that you know which direction you're arriving from, consult the appropriate STAR (Standard Terminal ARrival) and approach plates and plan your initial entry into the area shown. If you're flying into busy airspace, expect ATC to route you into the area via one of its "feeder" facilities.† If you're coming into Denver's Centennial Airport from the southeast, for example, you'll likely be

---

* An ATIS recording normally includes preferred runway information, and tells IFR arrivals which approaches are currently in use.

† A "feeder" fix is usually one of several VORTACS in the area. To find out more about preferred arrival routes in a specific area, telephone Flow Control at the regional ATC facility nearest your destination before planning your flight.

brought in over IOC (the Kiowa VORTAC) on the way. Note the position of that fix on the margins of the approach plate, and think about how you'll get from the feeder navaid into the initial approach phase. Plan your descent as well, including airspeed changes and checklists, and look over the airport diagram one more time (again, oriented to your expected arrival heading), so you'll know what to look for when (and if) you break out of the clouds.

Keep Your Ears Open

During your review, listen to the controllers to see how aircraft heading your way are vectored toward the approach. Most traffic will be sent along the same routes, so you can usually plan on getting similar treatment. As you get closer to Approach Control's airspace, the en route controller may even tell you which approach to expect. Such a notice isn't binding on the controller, of course, but is usually a reliable tidbit for planning the arrival.

Getting It All Together

Once you decide which approach or approaches you're most likely to receive, organize the appropriate plates and charts, preset any times in your countdown timer, make a note of the Minimum Descent Altitude (MDA) or Decision Height, and review the missed-approach procedure. The goal, as mentioned before, is to prepare yourself for the task ahead: getting your aircraft, your passengers, and yourself down through the weather and safely onto the runway.

PART FOUR

Arrival
Communications

CHAPTER 13

Approach Control

Who Are These People?

When you approach the airspace surrounding the destination airport, responsibility for your IFR flight transfers from the en route facility (Center) to the approach controller. Dedicated approach facilities (such as a TRACON) usually exist only near major civilian or military airports, or in crowded areas where IFR traffic converges on many airfields. If you're landing in a more remote setting, approach services are provided by one of the en route Center controllers.*

Approach Control is the entity responsible for all IFR traffic operating in and around its service area. Before you get too close to your destination airport, Center hands you

---

* For the purposes of this chapter, the terms "Approach" and "TRACON" refer to any facility providing approach control services to your flight, whether that facility is actually a TRACON or ARTCC.

off to Approach for final handling of your arrival. Although you may talk to more than one approach controller (in larger TRACON service areas), Approach itself is the last ATC facility you deal with prior to calling the destination tower for landing clearance.

Contacting Approach: WHO, WHY, and WHAT

The first radio call to Approach is almost as simple as the first call during any other handoff ("Hello, it's me, I'm level at X altitude"). There are, however, two major differences. For one thing, frequency congestion in terminal area often makes it difficult to make contact, even if time is running short on you. For another, you're a lot busier; you have approach charts to review, nav radios to set up, speed to bleed off, altitude to lose, and prelanding checklists to go through.

You already know *whom* you're calling: the facility that will help you descend and line up for the approach into your destination. The controller may be located far from the arrival airport, in a darkened radar room next to other TRACON controllers. In some places, however, Approach Control may be managed by someone in the control tower at your destination, looking at the same radar screen as the local (or tower) controller.

The *why* of calling Approach is also easy: You've been handed off, so they're expecting you. You're letting them know that you're entering their control area and are ready to be lined up for the approach. There are two things Approach wants you to tell them on your initial contact, one of which other controllers don't need: (*a*) your present altitude, of course, especially if you're still descending when you're handed off; and (*b*) whether you have the current ATIS information (if available) from the destination. Besides giving you the current weather advisory, ATIS also tells you what IFR approaches are currently in use. Once Approach knows that you have the information, they don't have to worry about explaining the upcoming procedure to you. So be sure you copy the current ATIS before getting too close to the arrival area (see chapter 12), and tell Approach you have the information when you call.

Contacting Approach: Sample Radio Calls

The last en route controller probably gave you descent instructions while you were still a fair distance out from the destination. When you are first cleared to descend from your en route altitude, listen briefly to the ATIS again to verify that the information you copied earlier is still valid. Once you actually arrive in the Approach's airspace, you may be too busy to recheck the information. If you and Center time the descent right, you will descend to an appropriate "transitional" altitude (one from which you can easily descend to the proper altitude for the instrument approach), just as you arrive at the TRACON service area boundary. In the examples below, assume you were cruising at 14,000 feet, and the last Center controller cleared you to descend and maintain 9,000 feet. As you descend through 11,500, Center hands you off to Approach the same way as to any other facility:

KING AIR THREE–EIGHT–NINER–KILO–
BRAVO, CONTACT DENVER APPROACH ON
ONE–ONE–NINER–POINT–THREE.

You should acknowledge this, like any other handoff, with a readback of the new frequency:

NINER–KILO–BRAVO, ROGER, ONE–ONE–
NINER–POINT–THREE, GOOD DAY.

Tune to the new frequency, wait for a break in the radio
traffic, then call in, giving your present altitude, the altitude you're descending to, and the name of the ATIS
information you copied:

DENVER APPROACH, KING AIR THREE–EIGHT–
NINER–KILO–BRAVO IS WITH YOU, OUT OF
ONE–ONE THOUSAND FOR NINER THOUSAND,
HAVE INFORMATION CHARLIE.

If Approach wants any more information, they'll ask for
it. Otherwise, they will acknowledge the call and issue any
further instructions:

KING AIR NINER–KILO–BRAVO, ROGER. DE-
SCEND AND MAINTAIN SEVEN THOUSAND
FIVE HUNDRED.

You respond to any new altitude assignments with a
readback:

OUT OF TEN THOUSAND EIGHT HUNDRED
FOR SEVEN THOUSAND FIVE HUNDRED,
NINER–KILO–BRAVO.

Vectors to the Approach

In most parts of the United States today, radar service is
available for at least a portion of the arrival phase. Where
it exists, ATC uses radar not only for actual radar approaches (ASR and PAR*) but also to provide radar vec-

---

* Airport Surveillance Radar or Precision Approach Radar approaches.

tors for other IFR approaches. Vectors speed up the flow of approach traffic by providing guidance directly onto the final approach segment of a published approach procedure. This guidance allows pilots to forego time-consuming initial or intermediate approach segments (such as procedure turns). The result is a quicker approach, allowing more aircraft to execute the approach over a given period. This keeps airspace around a busy airport less congested and offers shorter flight times (and better fuel economy) to arriving aircraft.

Altitude and vector assignments given to you during the approach carry the same weight as any clearance—you must stick to them until otherwise advised—but pilot accuracy is even more vital due to the increased density of traffic. Consider this image of TRACON airspace: Numerous aircraft arrive from all directions into a relatively small area at the same time, all seeking to line up and land on the same few runways. Approach must "funnel" all those aircraft into a small area, descend them to proper approach altitudes, and steer each onto the final approach with adequate horizontal and vertical separation. Into this taut situation, add the presence of other aircraft *departing* the same area (some in directions opposed to the arrivals). Departures are climbing out, arrivals are descending, and everyone is crossing each other's flight path at different altitudes. With all this in mind, it's easy to understand the importance of accurate heading and altitude control by every pilot in the area, including you. The *AIM* specifies that "pilots must not deviate from the headings issued by Approach Control," even if the present vector will take you beyond the inbound approach course (see "Cleared for the Approach," p. 139).

Expect the Visual

If your destination airport has two or more published instrument approaches, ATC will inform you which approach to expect, or that you will be vectored for a visual approach. You'll get this information from the ATIS or from a controller. If time is running out, however, and you don't know which approach is in use, it's kosher to ask someone.

Note, however, that information such as "expect the ——— approach . . ." is given to help you plan your arrival; but it is *not* an ATC clearance and thus is subject to change. You have not been cleared to fly the approach, so you can't start intercepting localizers or flying DME arcs until you're told to do so. If ATC ever tells you to expect an approach that you're unable to execute, it's your responsibility to inform ATC immediately.

Cancel IFR?

All IFR flight plans have to be "opened" and "closed," just like their VFR counterparts. Unlike VFR, however, the IFR flight plan is *automatically* opened and closed by ATC when you depart from (and arrive at) controlled airports. After you receive your IFR release, ATC's computers begin to watch for your aircraft to take off. When radar detects your presence, the flight plan is automatically activated. IFR flight plans are opened in this way anytime you fly into an area served by radar, even if you take off from an uncontrolled field. ATC also opens IFR flight plans when an aircraft reports entering controlled airspace in a nonradar environment.

As your flight continues, ATC's computers keep track of your progress by interrogating and following your transponder or through updates received from your position reports. When you land at an airport with an operating control tower, your flight plan is automatically closed.

The only time you have to close your IFR flight plan yourself is when you land at a field where there is no control tower (or if the tower is closed). If the weather forces you to execute a full instrument approach, you must contact ATC or Flight Service by telephone or radio after landing to close the flight plan (your failure to do so may result in the initiation of search-and-rescue efforts). Another option for closing your flight plan, available anytime you know you can land without the need for a full instrument approach, is to *cancel* IFR while you're still airborne and talking to ATC.

For example, suppose you're on an IFR flight plan on a clear day into a busy TCA, and you're landing at a satellite airport with no control tower. After you are sequenced into the area and have visual contact with the airport (assuming there are no low clouds), it is to everyone's benefit if you cancel your IFR flight plan with the approach controller. Canceling IFR serves to close your flight plan immediately and permits you to enter the pattern and land just as you would on any VFR flight, without having to take the time (or bear the expense) of a phone call to an FSS or ATC after landing. Likewise, you do the controller a favor by canceling IFR, because the airspace block you're occupying can then be released for use by another aircraft.

You can also cancel your IFR flight plan anytime you're flying in VFR conditions, provided you maintain VFR for the rest of the flight. The benefits of canceling IFR are mixed—you are free to fly any route you like (subject to airspace restrictions), and you aren't radar-monitored for accuracy of altitude and headings. On the other hand, you lose radar service (unless you request and receive VFR flight following), you don't have automatic permission to enter TCAs or other restricted areas (flights operating under an IFR clearance have permission to go where the clearance permits), and you have to worry about staying *completely* clear of clouds, even if that means huge deviations from your flight path.

The best time to cancel IFR, then, is when (*a*) you've descended into VFR conditions at the initial approach altitude for your destination, (*b*) you have the airport in sight, and (*c*) the airport doesn't have a control tower in operation. Canceling whenever you can in these situations will make things much easier for the folks at Approach Control. Note well, however, that canceling IFR is *never* mandatory, not even in good weather. If you are unfamiliar with the airport at which you're landing, or if visibility is poor due to haze or a low sun angle, you have the right to request a full instrument approach, even if the weather is clear. ATC may have to vector you around a little bit, but if shooting an approach helps you avoid any potential problems, it's worth the extra time and effort for all concerned.

To cancel your flight plan, simply tell the controller you want to cancel IFR. In this example, you are near the destination, with the airport in sight:

DENVER APPROACH, THIS IS KING AIR
THREE–EIGHT–NINER–KILO–BRAVO. I HAVE
THE AIRPORT IN SIGHT, PLEASE CANCEL MY
IFR FLIGHT PLAN.

Approach will usually respond with the following:

KING AIR NINER–KILO–BRAVO, THANK YOU.
IFR CANCELLATION RECEIVED. RADAR SER-
VICE IS TERMINATED, SQUAWK ONE–TWO–

ZERO–ZERO, CHANGE TO ADVISORY FRE-
QUENCY APPROVED.

As soon as ATC acknowledges cancellation of your flight
plan, the IFR portion of your flight is over. You *must* maintain VFR conditions throughout the rest of the flight, or
radio-file a new IFR flight plan if you later have to continue into IFR conditions.

Cleared for the Approach

After you are established on a segment of a published
instrument approach procedure at an appropriate altitude, ATC will issue your approach clearance. The clearance normally specifies an altitude or vector to reach the
final approach course, along with the name of the approach you should fly (e.g., "Cleared for ILS Runway
One–Three Right approach"). If the clearance lists no particular approach, you are cleared to execute any autho-
rized instrument approach procedure into the airport
(except a contact or visual approach).

Most approach clearances are delivered well before you
reach the final approach course or fix, and so include assignments of altitudes or vectors to get you there. Here is
a typical approach clearance:

KING AIR THREE–EIGHT–NINER–KILO–
BRAVO, YOU ARE FIVE MILES FROM THE
OUTER MARKER, TURN RIGHT HEADING
THREE—THREE–ZERO, MAINTAIN SEVEN
THOUSAND UNTIL ESTABLISHED ON THE LO-
CALIZER, CLEARED FOR THE ILS RUNWAY
THREE–SIX RIGHT APPROACH. CONTACT THE
TOWER AT THE MARKER, ONE–ONE–EIGHT–
POINT–ONE.

The clearance includes a lot of information to copy down, and deserves a clear readback of all important items:

NINER–KILO–BRAVO, ROGER. THREE–THREE–ZERO, MAINTAIN SEVEN THOUSAND UNTIL ON THE LOCALIZER, CLEARED ILS THREE–SIX RIGHT, TOWER AT THE MARKER.

At the same time you receive (and copy) that clearance, you should start complying with it. Turn right to the new heading *immediately,* beginning the turn even before you read back the clearance. Watch the CDI carefully for localizer intercept, and hold your altitude at 7,000 feet until you turn inbound onto the localizer. You were cleared to fly the *entire* approach, so you may intercept and follow the localizer, and descend as indicated in the published procedure (*after* you're established inbound on the localizer). Upon crossing over the outer marker, change to tower frequency as instructed. You won't get another handoff, and you don't need to report reaching the marker; just switch frequencies and call the tower. You're finally inbound on the approach and you won't be talking to Approach Control any more unless you execute a missed approach. The approach clearance gives you permission to do everything except land—and only the tower can clear you to do that.

What If I'm Not Cleared?

If you're nearing your destination and you haven't received any approach clearance, ask Approach when you should expect it. ATC may have overlooked you, or you might not have heard the clearance when it was first issued. The important thing is to speak up if you're not sure.

Be careful about turning to intercept the final approach course or beginning the approach procedure until you're *sure* you've been cleared. If you are flying a vector that will take you across the final approach course (such as a localizer), but you have not yet been told "intercept the localizer" or "cleared for the approach," ATC may be intentionally vectoring you across the course for traffic reasons. If you believe you should have been cleared to turn inbound, contact the controller before crossing the approach course and ask what you should do. As with any communication situation, it's perfectly acceptable to ask for more information or to ask ATC questions about your clearance or your flight. The only unacceptable practice in IFR communications is *failing* to verify vague or confusing instructions, or failing to speak up when things don't seem to be going according to plan.

As you become stabilized on the approach, contact the control tower—or switch to the Common Traffic Advisory Frequency (CTAF) when instructed to do so. You're almost on the ground, but until you are, you have to exercise your best IFR flying skills while juggling frequencies and controllers.

CHAPTER 14

Contact the Tower

Before You Go Barging In

Even though we don't usually think about it, most IFR flights begin and end in *VFR* conditions. Precious few instrument approaches are flown all the way to minimums; more often than not, you break out of the soup early, and the landing is flown visually. It's important, therefore, to remember that even though you're on an instrument flight plan—and the tower (if there is one) is holding open a big block of space for you—you must still comply with *VFR* arrival procedures when you're in the vicinity of the traffic pattern. You should approach the pattern for a 45°-angle entry into the downwind leg (when possible), and be on a constant lookout for other traffic. If VFR conditions exist at the field and there is other traffic in the area, fly a circling approach in the VFR traffic pattern. If there are VFR pilots operating in the area, they will hear you call on the radio that you're "inbound on the XYZ approach," but they may not know what that means. It's important for them to know where you're coming from, and at what altitude. Next time you're en route into an airport on an instrument procedure, then, bear in mind that there might be other pilots who need to know what you're doing and who will expect you to fly the pattern just like everyone else.

Tower versus CTAF

When landing at a controlled field, the control tower is the final ATC facility you have to contact while you're still airborne. If your destination has no tower, or if the tower is closed, the *approach* controller is your final radio link to the ATC system. As mentioned before, you may choose to cancel your IFR flight plan with approach (or any controller), after which you proceed according to visual flight rules. If you continue IFR into the airport vicinity, you must conduct the flight under instrument flight rules, and controllers must provide you with IFR sequencing and separation.*

When you call the tower for permission to land or take off, you are talking to the "local" controller. There may be several other positions operating in the cab (the glass-enclosed control room at the top of a control tower), such as ground control, clearance delivery/ATIS, and even an approach controller (if approach isn't being handled by a

---

* This is one reason why canceling IFR makes you a good guy in ATC's eyes. As long as you are still on an IFR flight plan, controllers at the airport have to maintain IFR separation between you and other arrivals and departures, even if the weather is severely clear and you're lined up directly on the runway. If you cancel IFR once you are comfortably in the pattern, the local controller can space traffic more closely, and flow management is made easier for everyone.

local TRACON facility). But when Approach tells you to "contact the tower," the local controller is the person responsible for your flight until you're on the ground and off the active runway. After the handoff to the tower, you will be cleared to land (eventually), and when you do so your IFR flight plan is automatically closed.

If the destination airport lacks a control tower (or if the tower is closed, as is often the case late at night), you break radio contact with ATC and become your own controller for the rest of the flight. Instead of handing you off to the tower, Approach will give you a final approach clearance and say, "Change to advisory frequency approved." After acknowledging the instruction, you switch your comm radio to the CTAF for the airport, listen briefly for radio traffic, and then broadcast your intentions in the blind. You continue to fly the published approach exactly as you were told by Approach, and land if the weather is above minimums. After you park, you contact an FSS or ATC by phone to advise them that you have landed and to request cancellation of your IFR flight plan.

This chapter first explains radio procedures for calling an active control tower, and then examines procedures used when broadcasting on a CTAF.

Calling the Tower: WHO, WHY, and WHAT

In the initial radio call after Approach hands you off, you should tell the controller who you are and what you're doing (flying a specific approach), even though the controller *should* already know. As you have seen, the *who, why,* and *what* questions are easily answered with most radio calls. This is certainly true when calling the tower.

Who is *local* control, addressed by the name of the facility and the word "tower" (e.g., "San Francisco Tower," "Denver Tower," "Teterboro Tower"). This controller is responsible for traffic landing or taking off from the active runways of the airfield, as well as for aircraft operations within the airport traffic area. This is the only person who can clear you to land at a controlled field, so you *must* make contact and receive permission before landing, even if you already received an approach clearance. The *why* is clear—you're calling to get permission to finish flying the published approach procedure and land at the airport.

The *what* aspect of this call has two parts: You should tell the tower (*a*) who and where you are, and (*b*) what you're doing. Specifically, you should identify yourself and state what approach you're flying and where you are on the procedure. If all is going according to plan, the tower controller already knows where you are, sees you on radar (or has your aircraft in sight, weather permitting), and knows what approach you're flying. But, as emphasized earlier, the name of the game in communications is *verifying* everything to avoid error or confusion. This is especially true during instrument approaches, when you're flying ever-closer to the ground, and things are happening fast. If you call in and tell the tower you're "inbound from the marker on the ILS Two–Six Left," but the controller expected you on the VOR-DME Runway 26 Right, your initial call will warn of the confusion and might save the day. A simpler call, such as "inbound on the approach" is accurate, but it doesn't provide adequate verification of your intentions.

Calling the Tower: Sample Radio Calls

The initial callup should reflect your position and where you are on the procedure:

PHOENIX TOWER, CITATION THREE–EIGHT–
NINER–KILO–BRAVO, WITH YOU AT FOUR
THOUSAND, FOWLE INTERSECTION INBOUND
ON THE ILS RUNWAY EIGHT RIGHT.

Or:

PHOENIX TOWER, CITATION THREE–EIGHT–
NINER–KILO–BRAVO WITH YOU AT FOUR
THOUSAND, ENTERING LEFT BASE ON THE
POWER PLANT VISUAL APPROACH FOR RUN-
WAY TWO-SIX LEFT.

Stating the obvious (that you're on the "visual approach") is yet another way to double-check what you're
doing with what you're *supposed* to be doing, and to remind
the tower controller who you are and where you are.

Assuming the tower expects you, you'll hear some sort
of acknowledgment, usually followed by a clearance to
land:

CITATION NINER–KILO–BRAVO, PHOENIX
TOWER. ROGER. REPORT THE MARKER,
CLEARED TO LAND RUNWAY EIGHT RIGHT.

Or:

CITATION NINER–KILO–BRAVO, PHOENIX
TOWER. ROGER. YOU ARE NUMBER TWO BE-
HIND A BOEING SEVEN–TWO–SEVEN, CON-
TINUE APPROACH TO RUNWAY TWO-SIX
LEFT.

Acknowledge and repeat landing clearances *without fail.*
If you never acknowledge any other instructions (although
you should), you *must* repeat every takeoff or landing clearance given by a control tower. The potential for harm
(such as an unscheduled meeting with another aircraft) is

so great, and the burden on you is so small, that there is no excuse for not repeating with something simple and complete:

CLEARED TO LAND EIGHT RIGHT, NINER–KILO–BRAVO.

Be very careful here: Just because you were cleared for the approach earlier, you *do not* have a landing clearance if the control zone is in effect (i.e., if the tower is operating). Don't continue to fly an approach and land without permission to do so from the tower. If you don't get a landing clearance after contacting the tower, *ask for one.* Perhaps the controller is releasing other traffic, or perhaps you didn't hear your clearance when it was issued. Again, the important thing is to *ask* rather than *assume.*

Likewise, after your initial call to the tower, don't fall prey to the common human tendency to "hear what you expect to hear." In other words, don't convince yourself that the tower cleared you to land just because they acknowledged your presence. While you're busy flying down the glideslope and configuring for landing, you might forget to maintain clear communications with the tower, but you can't land without receiving permission. Even though the tower says, "Roger, you are number two . . . ," you can't just land after the airplane ahead of you unless the controller okays it. Don't kid yourself into thinking, "Well, she probably *meant* that I was cleared to land." *Never fly onto or off a controlled runway without an express clearance to do so. If you aren't sure, ask.* If you don't get a clearance and it's getting late, declare a missed approach and go around. A little extra fuel or extra rental time on the Hobbs meter is a small price to pay when you consider the possible result of landing without a clearance.

CTAF and Uncontrolled Airports

For those not used to operations around uncontrolled airfields,* proper use of the Common Traffic Advisory Frequency may be a mystery. The function of the CTAF is the same as the tower frequency at the busy airport—management of departing and landing traffic. But unlike a control tower, on CTAF the pilots control themselves. When you make a call on the CTAF, you "broadcast your intentions," telling the world at large what you *plan* to do.† Sometimes a private FBO operator or fuel desk offers Unicom services on the same frequency, but this isn't an FAA controller; it's just someone who will provide wind and traffic information to anyone who asks.

You don't need permission from any ATC facility to land or take off from an uncontrolled field, but wise pilots always state their intentions on the CTAF—and listen for the intentions of others—before flying onto or off the runway. So *whom* you are calling on the CTAF when flying an approach varies from flight to flight. You may be calling no one, or you may be informing a patternful of student pilots that you are inbound to the area.

Although many pilots assume radio communications are easier to manage at uncontrolled airports, the reverse is often true. Even though you don't have to report to Clearance Delivery, Ground Control, and the tower when

---

* As used in this section, the term "uncontrolled airfield" refers to airports where there is no control tower *and* those tower-equipped airports where the tower is not in operation.

† Standard radio calls are directed to some specific pilot, controller, or facility. "Broadcasts," on the other hand, are intended to reach any interested listener on the frequency. ATC commonly broadcasts "news" items such as SIGMETs, AIRMETs, and wind shear alerts. Your call on the CTAF is a broadcast because you don't know who, if anyone, may be operating in the area and/or listening on the frequency.

the CTAF is in use, you face an even tougher challenge: You must listen to *every* radio call in your area, not just the calls which begin with your aircraft ID. In other words, when you're approaching to land at a controlled field, you can "tune out" and disregard all tower transmissions except the ones addressed to you specifically. With a CTAF, on the other hand, you have to pay attention to *all* broadcasts and make sure you know where all other aircraft in the area are and what they're doing. In addition, you have sole responsibility for giving yourself "clearance" to land or take off because there's no controller in the tower watching out behind you or providing separation in the pattern. The net effect is a heavier workload. You have to listen to everyone, call out your own intentions periodically, and still fly the instrument approach procedure into (usually) a smaller airport with no controllers on the air.

Calling on CTAF: WHO, WHY, and WHAT

The reason you broadcast on the CTAF is *as a precaution.* The purpose of the frequency is to provide an open line for pilots operating in or around the area to tell each other where they are and what they are doing. When you are cleared for the approach by ATC and told "change to advisory frequency approved," you switch to the CTAF and call in so that others know you're coming.

It should be obvious *what* your audience wants to hear from you on the CTAF: Any pilots operating in the area will be interested in knowing of your presence, so you need to advise them where you are, your altitude, what approach you're flying, and whether you intend to land or are just practicing an approach.

When ATC okays your change to advisory frequency,

tune it in and listen for a few seconds. In many cases, you'll hear weak broadcasts from other aircraft, *operating at other airports,* using the same frequency. This is the real headache for those who depend on CTAFs or Unicom frequencies; only a few comm frequencies are reserved for such use, so it's not unusual for several airports within a 100-mile radius to use the same frequency for traffic advisories. The result is severe congestion on these frequencies and confusion as to who is talking to whom, and at which airport. You can, however, minimize the risk of confusion by naming the airfield where you're operating at the beginning *and the end* of all CTAF broadcasts.

A Word About the "Other Pilot"

An important skill in all flying, particularly in instrument flight, is "flying smart." Remember when you took driver's ed in school? You learned to *look* for signs of trouble, to *expect* trouble, and to *plan* how to avoid it. You were taught to assume that the other driver was going to do something stupid, and to be ready for it. This is known as "defensive driving," and it keeps you out of trouble when things beyond your control go awry. Whenever you fly (but especially when flying in IFR conditions without ATC's supervision—in other words, when executing an approach into an uncontrolled airport), you must *fly* defensively. If you assume someone will make a mistake, you're better equipped to handle it when they do.

When flying an approach in IFR conditions into an airport where no one is supervising the traffic, you may come face-to-face with another aircraft unless you both know what the other is doing. This means you must clearly state, *at all times,* your location and altitude, your direction of flight (or the approach you're on), and any other information another pilot might need to know to stay out of your way. Likewise, you should monitor broadcasts by all other pilots and be sure you know where they are and what they're doing.

In a typical CTAF communications setting, several pilots may operate in the same area for a period of several minutes (e.g., students practicing touch-and-go landings in closed traffic while several aircraft inbound for landing arrive in the area). If traffic is light, the aircraft may make all their broadcasts to the public at large. Sometimes, however, when you hear another pilot make a call, you may wish to communicate directly with that other aircraft. In such a situation, you should call out to the aircraft, using the identifier its pilot used; identify yourself; and speak directly to the other pilot. So long as it doesn't degenerate into idle chatter, one-to-one communication between pilots greatly enhances safety in the absence of a tower controller.

For example, suppose you are flying inbound to your local airport, and you hear a Mooney on the same CTAF advise that it is "on a right base for Runway Three–Five." Two minutes later, you arrive in the traffic area, see the airport, and enter the pattern for Runway 35. Besides announcing your own presence, you need to locate the Mooney and find out whether it is still flying, practicing, or clear of the runway. If you can't see the Mooney, and you haven't heard from it in a few minutes, just call in the blind to the pilot:

MOONEY OPERATING AT SWAMP FIELD, THIS IS CITATION THREE–EIGHT–NINER–KILO– BRAVO. WHAT IS YOUR POSITION?

If you can establish a meaningful dialogue with another pilot when the two of you are operating in close proximity, your chances of an unplanned encounter are greatly reduced.

Calling on CTAF: Sample Radio Calls

After switching frequencies and verifying that no one else is broadcasting, announce your presence and intentions. Suppose you are flying into Scottsdale Municipal in Scottsdale, Arizona, after the tower is closed:

> SCOTTSDALE TRAFFIC, CITATION THREE–EIGHT–NINER–KILO–BRAVO, GELTS INTERSECTION AT FOUR THOUSAND, INBOUND ON VOR–ALPHA APPROACH, SCOTTSDALE.

Or, if you're flying the visual approach:

> SCOTTSDALE TRAFFIC, CITATION THREE–EIGHT–NINER–KILO–BRAVO, ENTERING LEFT DOWNWIND AT TWO THOUSAND FIVE HUNDRED ON THE VISUAL APPROACH FOR RUNWAY TWO-ONE, SCOTTSDALE.

Now suppose you are flying into an airport such as La Plata County Airport in Durango, Colorado. Durango has no tower, but the approach plate indicates there is a Unicom frequency in operation. It's a safe practice always to ask for an airport advisory on Unicom when announcing your presence for the first time:

> DURANGO UNICOM, CITATION THREE–EIGHT–NINER–KILO–BRAVO, IRISS MARKER AT ONE–ONE THOUSAND, OUTBOUND ON ILS/DME RUNWAY TWO APPROACH, REQUEST AIRPORT ADVISORY.

If anyone is on duty, you should receive a report on prevailing winds and the current altimeter setting:

CITATION NINER–KILO–BRAVO, DURANGO UNICOM. WIND TWO–THREE–ZERO AT ONE– FIVE, PREFERRED RUNWAY TWO–ZERO, AL– TIMETER THREE–ZERO–ONE–ONE.

For all remaining communications, use the Unicom/ CTAF frequency as you would any other CTAF—to an- nounce your position and intentions, without addressing calls to the Unicom operator.

Recall that CTAF broadcasts include the name of the facility *twice*—at both the beginning and the end. This is redundant but, like flying with two comm radios, it is a small price to pay, given the safety margin it allows. Any- one who has spent much time flying around uncontrolled fields knows that it's tough to fly your own aircraft and concentrate on everyone else's broadcasts at the same time. You may be busy flying the approach and vaguely hear someone state they are in "left closed traffic, touch- and-go, Runway Two–Two." If that's all you hear, and several airports in the area use the same CTAF, you don't know at *which* airport Runway 22 is, so you don't know where that aircraft is. If, on the other hand, you hear ". . . touch-and go, Runway Two, Durango," you're on notice that someone is operating in the pattern where you're going, and the two of you have to be on the look- out for each other.

After your initial radio call, continue the approach and listen carefully for indications of other aircraft operating in the vicinity. Whether you hear anyone else or not, con- tinue to announce your progress right up until landing. Even when there are no other aircraft in sight and not a soul on the radio, keep telling the world what you're up to. Other pilots may arrive in the area or start up their aircraft on the ground, and they may not have heard you the first

time. It's your job to keep anyone on the frequency updated on your position.

On the full ILS/DME procedure at Durango, you execute the procedure turn at or above 10,000 feet. Anytime
you execute a full approach with a procedure turn, two
good opportunities to make CTAF reports are when you
begin and end the procedure turn:

> DURANGO TRAFFIC, CITATION THREE–
> EIGHT–NINER–KILO–BRAVO AT ONE–ZERO
> THOUSAND, FIVE MILES SOUTHWEST, PROCE-
> DURE TURN OUTBOUND ON THE ILS/DME
> RUNWAY TWO APPROACH, DURANGO.

Followed by:

> DURANGO TRAFFIC, CITATION NINER–KILO–
> BRAVO IS AT ONE–ZERO THOUSAND, SIX
> SOUTHWEST, PROCEDURE TURN INBOUND
> ON THE ILS/DME RUNWAY TWO APPROACH,
> DURANGO.

Each of these calls updates anyone on the frequency of
your progress and warns newcomers to the area that you
are in the middle of the approach procedure.

As you track the localizer inbound and reach HINDY
intersection, you descend to and maintain 9,500 feet until
glideslope intercept, then fly the ILS. The final approach
fix is the outer marker (IRISS). The middle marker (at 0.4
DME) is the missed-approach point, and even at a ground-
speed of 150 knots, you have nearly three minutes before
you reach the Missed Approach Point (MAP) from IRISS.
With so much time remaining before you reach the airport, you can easily make at least one more broadcast before you get there:

DURANGO TRAFFIC, CITATION THREE–
EIGHT–NINER–KILO–BRAVO IS THREE MILES
SOUTHWEST, INBOUND ON THE ILS/DME RUN-
WAY TWO APPROACH, DURANGO.

Airport in Sight

If you don't have a requisite part of the runway environment in sight at the MAP, you must immediately fly a
missed approach (see p. 157). If you break out of clouds
and have the right landmarks in sight, however, enter the
pattern for a normal landing, using simple CTAF broadcasts (remember that this example assumes the winds favor a circle-to-land at pattern altitude):

DURANGO TRAFFIC, CITATION THREE–
EIGHT–NINER–KILO–BRAVO AT EIGHT THOU-
SAND, ENTERING A LEFT DOWNWIND FOR
RUNWAY TWO–ZERO, DURANGO.

Fly a normal pattern (keeping the runway in sight), and
make a call when you turn base:

DURANGO TRAFFIC, CITATION THREE–
EIGHT–NINER–KILO–BRAVO TURNING LEFT
BASE FOR RUNWAY TWO–ZERO, DURANGO.

And then again when you turn onto final approach:

DURANGO TRAFFIC, CITATION THREE–
EIGHT–NINER–KILO–BRAVO ON A ONE–MILE
FINAL, RUNWAY TWO–ZERO, DURANGO.

When you fly the pattern (or line up for a straight-in
landing, as you could have done if the winds had favored
Runway 2), you are close enough to the airport to *see* what's
going on as well as hear it on the CTAF. The prudent pilot

keeps an eye on the ramp, the approach and departure ends of the runway(s), and the entire pattern area (above, at, and below normal pattern altitudes) while circling to land. Watch for aircraft movement on the ground, especially aircraft taxiing toward (or on) the runway. Scan the downwind, base, and final areas for traffic on *both* sides of the runway (in case someone else is flying right traffic while you're flying left). Such vigilance will help avoid conflicts when other aircraft don't hear you, or when they operate in the area without a radio at all (which is legal, but not necessarily advisable). Be especially careful as you turn final. Is someone departing downwind, straight into you? Is this a small field where back-taxiing on the runway is necessary?

Stabilize the final approach, then make one more radio call before crossing the fence:

DURANGO TRAFFIC, CITATION THREE–EIGHT–NINER–KILO–BRAVO ON A QUARTER-MILE FINAL RUNWAY TWO–ZERO, DURANGO.

After touchdown, report your movements on the CTAF until you're off the runway. Remember, someone else may be inbound on an approach behind you.

DURANGO TRAFFIC, CITATION THREE–EIGHT–NINER–KILO–BRAVO IS CLEAR OF THE ACTIVE RUNWAY TWO–ZERO, DURANGO.

Your last act of communication with ATC comes after you park the aircraft and shut it down. Unless you canceled IFR while in flight (which you cannot do if the weather isn't VFR), you must notify ATC that you have landed. From any telephone, notify the nearest FSS, TRACON, or ARTCC that you have just landed and wish to cancel an IFR flight plan. The specialist on the other end will take the necessary information from you, and that should be the end of it. Before you get off the phone, however, ask for your contact's full name. Many pilots tell of having closed a flight plan by phone (VFR or IFR) and later hearing that someone was frantically searching for them. Ask for the name of the FAA employee and write it on your flight log (e.g., "Flight plan closed with Controller X at Albuquerque FSS, 3:15 p.m. local time"). Chances are you'll never have to defend your actions to the FAA, but getting a name is cheap insurance.

As an instrument-rated pilot, you already know that you don't even get to the "flying the pattern" part of CTAF communications unless you are able to complete the approach. As soon as you reach the MAP, you must have the runway environment in sight or execute an immediate missed approach.

Missed Approach

At a Controlled Airport: Flying the missed approach when the control tower is operating calls for simple radio procedures. You've already been talking to the tower, so you just hit the push-to-talk button and report:

PHOENIX TOWER, CITATION THREE–EIGHT–NINER–KILO–BRAVO, MISSED APPROACH.

At the same time, begin the missed-approach procedure without hesitation (for the ILS Runway 8 at Phoenix, the procedure is a straight-ahead climb to 5,000 feet, then direct to the Salt River VORTAC). The tower should respond with instructions:

CITATION NINER–KILO–BRAVO, ROGER, CONTINUE CLIMB AND CONTACT APPROACH, ONE–TWO–ZERO–POINT–SEVEN.

Acknowledge the handoff as soon as you're safely squared away in your climb (power set, positive rate of climb, gear and flaps up) and call Approach:

PHOENIX APPROACH, CITATION THREE–EIGHT–NINER–KILO–BRAVO WITH YOU OUT OF THREE THOUSAND FOR FIVE, MISSED APPROACH.

In all likelihood, Phoenix Tower will have already notified Approach that you were on the missed approach, so they'll be expecting you.

At an Uncontrolled Airport: If you're flying an approach into an uncontrolled field, the communications required for a missed approach are slightly more complicated. First, you have to announce the missed approach on the CTAF:

DURANGO TRAFFIC, CITATION THREE–EIGHT–NINER–KILO–BRAVO, MISSED APPROACH FROM THE ILS/DME RUNWAY TWO APPROACH, DURANGO.

You must state the name of the approach you just missed (here, "ILS/DME Runway 2"), because the missed-approach procedures are often different for different approaches, and your broadcast should tell others where you are and where you're going.

Next, you have to switch back to the last ATC frequency you were using (aren't you glad you have it written down?) and call Approach Control back, explaining your situation:

DENVER CENTER, CITATION THREE–EIGHT–NINER–KILO–BRAVO WITH YOU OUT OF SEVEN THOUSAND FIVE HUNDRED FOR ONE–ZERO THOUSAND, MISSED APPROACH.

Approach Control's Response: Whether you pop up on a missed approach from a controlled or uncontrolled airport, the approach controller will acknowledge your call and ask your intentions:

CITATION NINER–KILO–BRAVO, DENVER CENTER, ROGER. SAY INTENTIONS.

ATC has to know if you want to try another approach, proceed to your alternate, hold for a while in hopes that the weather will break, or any other option you may be considering. Let the controller know as quickly as possible what you want to do. If you have reason to believe the weather is improving, you may want to go back for another bite at the apple right away:

CENTER, NINER–KILO–BRAVO WOULD LIKE TO FLY THE ILS/DME RUNWAY TWO AP-PROACH AGAIN.

If some temporary phenomenon (such as a localized snow shower or wind shear) caused the missed approach, perhaps you should consider holding:

CENTER, NINER–KILO–BRAVO, WE'D LIKE TO HOLD BRIEFLY AT DURANGO VOR THEN ATTEMPT THE APPROACH AGAIN.

If, on the other hand, the fuel gauges and your common sense tell you it's time to head for clearer weather, don't kill time loitering in the area:

CENTER, NINER–KILO–BRAVO, WE'LL PRO-CEED TO FARMINGTON AT THIS TIME.

Depending upon what you request, ATC may issue vectors, holding instructions, or a new clearance to another airport. Be ready to copy and read back the instructions, then get yourself mentally back on track and continue with the flight.

Coping with the Missed Approach: **Radio** communications after a missed approach are the same as any other phase of IFR flight: You listen carefully to the controllers, communicate your intentions and your needs clearly, and follow ATC's instructions to the extent possible. From the moment you declare a missed approach, the flight proceeds as it did when you first entered Approach Control's airspace, i.e., you'll receive vectors or other instructions, and you'll fly another approach or go to your alternate. Unless you're running low on fuel, flying a missed approach should be no more exciting than any other part of the flight. Missed approaches aren't normally emergencies; they are delays. Just keep flying the airplane, keep communicating, and be patient. If you planned your flight carefully, you should have ample fuel to hold for a time and then try again or go to your alternate.

Wrapping It All Up

As you know, the controllers at a tower-controlled field will automatically cancel your IFR flight plan when they see you land. ATC will also cancel the flight plan during the flight (if you request it), or when you phone Flight Service after landing at an uncontrolled destination. Whatever the circumstances, be sure you close your flight plan in one way or another. If, after a flight, you're not sure whether your flight plan was canceled or not, call the nearest FSS or ATC facility and ask. They will look up your aircraft's tail number on the computer and make sure the plan isn't still active.

Contact Ground Control

After landing at an airport with a separate ground control frequency, your communications responsibility continues until you shut down the aircraft. When rolling out after landing, the tower controller will usually tell you to exit the runway at some specific location, and clear you to contact ground control:

CITATION NINER–KILO–BRAVO, EXIT VIA TAXIWAY CHARLIE–SIX IF ABLE, CONTACT GROUND POINT–NINER WHEN CLEAR OF THE RUNWAY.

The response is a readback, just like any other:

NINER–KILO–BRAVO, ROGER. CHARLIE–SIX IF ABLE, GROUND POINT–NINER WHEN CLEAR.

This is a fairly simple (and typical) "contact ground" radio exchange, but there are several important things to consider with such instructions:

(a) It's easy to relax your vigilance immediately after landing, but you must be careful to follow the tower's instructions *exactly*. Many mishaps occur as aircraft trundle around on the ramp and taxiways, so be sure you write down the instructions, watch where you're going, and listen carefully.

(b) Second, you were told to turn off onto Taxiway C–6, *if able*, and this means you may use your discretion and keep rolling beyond C–6 if the aircraft is still going too fast, if braking action is poor, if you landed long, or if taking the turn would be unsafe for any other reason. If you do opt to continue to a later taxiway, however, the tower will appreciate it if you will respond by saying "Tower, Niner–Kilo–Bravo unable to exit Charlie–Six." Controllers aren't normally upset when you're unable to comply with a request, but you can make their lives easier if you keep them informed of any such inability.

(c) The controller said, "Contact ground Point–Niner . . ." instead of giving you a complete frequency. Most ground control frequencies are assigned within the 121 MHz band (between 121.0 and 121.9 MHz), so controllers are taught to say "Point–Niner" for 121.9, "Point–Six" for 121.6, etc.

(d) Note also that the controller said to *contact* ground control. Normally, when you are told to contact ground, you make an introductory radio call to them after clearing the runway and tell them who you are, where you are, and where you wish to taxi. Occasionally, however, if only one controller is working both the tower and ground frequencies (a common situation at smaller fields or at low traffic periods), you will be instructed to *"monitor* ground" instead of "contact ground." In that case, you switch to the ground control frequency when off the runway, and then taxi to your destination while *just listening* on the ground control frequency and keeping your eyes peeled for other aircraft. You are not required to establish contact with ground control, but you monitor the frequency so that the controller can contact you with instructions should a conflict arise.

(e) The instruction to contact ground control specifically included the words "when clear of the runway." This means just what it says: You must remain on the tower frequency until you slow down, turn onto a taxiway, and your entire aircraft is clear of the active runway. *Do not* switch over during the rollout. The tower is the entity that controls the active runways, and you *must* remain in contact with the tower until clear of their turf. After you're clear, don't taxi into any new intersections or across any other runways without clearance from ground control. Come to a halt if necessary, and wait until you can break in on the ground control frequency. So long as you're clear of an active runway, you aren't likely to be involved in a collision if you sit still.

Your first call to ground control is a simple, "here I am" message:

PHOENIX GROUND, CITATION THREE–EIGHT–NINER–KILO–BRAVO AT CHARLIE–SIX, REQUEST TAXI TO [destination].

Sometimes, ground control simply responds, "Taxi as requested." In that case, you should take the most direct route (via taxiways only, please) that will keep you clear of aircraft gates, run-up areas, or active runways. Normally, however, ground control at a large airport will give you some explicit instructions. In this situation, you're receiving a clearance, and—like any other clearance—you should copy it down and read it back (if you don't want to copy it down, try tracing your route on the airport diagram in pencil):

CITATION NINER–KILO–BRAVO, PROCEED NORTH TO TAXIWAY BRAVO, THEN WEST TO FBO PARKING.

Your readback should be short and clear:

NINER–KILO–BRAVO, ROGER. NORTH TO BRAVO THEN WEST TO PARK.

From now until you park at the FBO or hangar, you may be tempted to busy yourself in the cockpit by putting away chart binders, retracting flaps, draining coffee cups, and loosening your seat belt. But remember that you are still operating an aircraft, and you must still be in contact with ground control. Accordingly, you should ignore distractions, keep your eyes scanning outside, and carefully monitor the ground control frequency for further instructions and to hear who else is taxiing in your vicinity. Ground control will not usually call again unless other aircraft are moving near you, or if they need to modify your earlier taxi clearance. Thus, once you've reached your parking location, no further communications are necessary.

PART FIVE

Further Considerations

CHAPTER 15

Controller Authority vs. Pilot Authority

When you fly IFR, you and the air traffic controllers along your route communicate with each other. This communication, and the way pilots and ATC interact to make the IFR system work, are the subjects of this book. Yet if you are to understand the context in which you and the controllers share responsibility for safe aircraft operations, you have to understand the authority under which you both operate. In other words, you have to know where controller authority ends—and yours begins.

The Foundations of Authority

The authority of both pilots and air traffic controllers in the United States derives primarily from the rules imposed by the FAA under a mandate from Congress. These rules, referred to collectively as the FARs (the Federal Aviation Regulations), are published by the government under Title 14 of the Code of Federal Regulations (CFR). The *Air Traffic Control Handbook* is the FAA's primary guidebook for controllers. In addition to these sources, most states have civil and/or criminal statutes that restrict aircraft operations and prescribe penalties for unsafe or trespassory flights.

You don't have to be an attorney to be held responsible for knowledge of the law. Many have heard the expression "ignorance of the law is no excuse." The rule certainly holds true for flight operations in the United States: It is your responsibility to comply with all statutes and regulations, whether state or federal, affecting your flight. The authorities assume you know and will comply with all of these rules, and you can expect to be held accountable for any violation (even if you didn't know you were breaking the law).

This isn't to say, however, that you should live in constant fear of an FAR violation every time you remove the tie-downs and start the engines. It simply means that a responsible pilot will devote some time and effort to knowing the restrictions and requirements imposed by the FARs, and by statute, when planning and carrying out a flight.

If you're a licensed pilot, then you already know the substance of many FARs. They governed how your flight training was conducted and how many hours you needed to take your first flight test. The regulations make the distinction between weather that is just hazy and conditions that are really IFR. They prescribe minimum equipment for certain operations and prevent private pilots from carrying passengers for hire. One of the best investments for your aviation reference library is to spend ten or fifteen dollars for the current *AIM/FAR* at least once a year. This is a volume combining the latest updates of both publications, usually in a ready-reference format. The *AIM* section is a gold mine of useful flight information, and the *FAR* section gives you the latest revisions in the laws that govern your flight activities.

FAR Part 91, "General Operating and Flight Rules," provides the basic operating rules for most flight activities. A complete review and understanding of the FARs is far beyond the scope of this book. Nevertheless, there is one regulation in Part 91 that you should commit to memory. It is the very foundation for your authority as pilot in command and, as such, you must keep it foremost in your mind when operating an aircraft. It is 14 CFR Section 91.3, aptly titled "Responsibility and Authority of the Pilot In Command." The first two paragraphs of this section state:

(a) The pilot in command of an aircraft is *directly responsible for,* and is *the final authority as to,* the operation of that aircraft.

(b) In an *in-flight emergency* requiring immediate action, the pilot in command *may deviate from any rule* of this part to the extent required to meet that emergency.

[Amended 1989, effective August 18, 1990 (emphasis added).]

Paragraph (c) requires a pilot to send a written report to the FAA (if requested) explaining any rule deviation made under the emergency authority of Section 91.3(b).

Let's look at these rules again. Paragraph (a) may be thought of as the ultimate arbiter of responsibility. It says simply that you, as pilot in command of an aircraft, are the one person whose empennage is on the line when things don't go right. In other words, the buck stops at Section 91.3(a). Responsibility for every flight—and for any rule violation or mishap—rests squarely on your shoulders. Every time the NTSB cites "pilot error" as contributing to or causing an accident, it is Section 91.3(a) that buttresses that finding. The pilot is the ultimate authority, so *any* mishap is arguably the pilot's fault.

Paragraph (b), in contrast, is a sort of ultimate loophole for all the rules contained in Part 91. If you study every section of the FARs, you will not find another paragraph that is so universally adaptable to any situation. The message of Section 91.3(b) is crystal-clear: when trouble arises, and immediate action is required on your part to "meet" the crisis, you may deviate from *any* rule of Part 91 in order to handle the situation.

The effect of Section 91.3(b) is to absolve the pilot in command from liability for any rule violation under Part 91 when the following circumstances exist:

1. there is an *in-flight emergency* requiring *immediate action* ("emergency" is defined as a *distress* or *urgency* condition—see footnote, page 181);

2. the course of action necessary to *meet* that emergency and maintain the safety of the flight requires the pilot in command to deviate from a rule under Part 91; and

3. the pilot deviates from said rule(s) only to the extent needed to meet the emergency.*

---

* Although the rule doesn't specifically say so, the state of the law is such that even if you are *wrong* about having an in-flight emergency at the time you exercise your Section 91.3(b) authority (i.e., if it later turns out there was no fire), a rule infraction should still be forgiven if your belief in the emergency was sincere and reasonable under the circumstances. In other words, if you *honestly believe* you're in trouble and act accordingly, Section 91.3(b) will ordinarily protect you.

Application of Section 91.3(b)

Section 91.3(b) applies to many situations during IFR operations. A pilot may exercise this authority to deviate around a thunderstorm, climb above icing conditions, land on a road or field if the engine quits, or descend below ILS decision height if there's a fire on board. In the context of IFR *communications*, however, there is one primary situation in which you may need to exercise your emergency authority: refusing to accept, or deviating from, IFR clearances.

One fundamental rule of IFR communication is little-known to pilots: Because you (and not the controller) are ultimately responsible for the operation of your aircraft, you have an absolute right to *refuse* any ATC clearance if it would require deviation from a rule or regulation, would place the aircraft in danger, or is vague, ambiguous, or beyond the capabilities of the pilot or the machine. *Until you accept a clearance, you are not required to comply with it, provided your refusal to accept the clearance is based on one of the reasons stated above.*

The *AIM* and Pilot/Controller Authority

Paragraphs 260 and 401 of the *AIM* (below) explain the relationship between pilot and controller authority, and indicate just who is the final authority when a clearance conflicts with a rule or with safety requirements. Under these requirements, you have an obligation to speak up when you believe you have reason to refuse a clearance:

260. *CLEARANCE*

(a) A clearance issued by ATC is predicated on known traffic and known physical airport conditions. An

ATC clearance means an authorization by ATC, for the purpose of preventing collision between known aircraft, for an aircraft to proceed under specified conditions within controlled airspace. *It is not authorization for a pilot to deviate from any rule, regulation, or minimum altitude, nor to conduct unsafe operation of [the] aircraft.*

(b) [Cites FAR Section 91.3 (a) —The pilot in command is the ultimate authority for the operation of an aircraft.] If ATC issues a clearance that would cause a pilot to deviate from a rule or regulation, or in the pilot's opinion, would place the aircraft in jeopardy, *it is the pilot's responsibility to request an amended clearance.* Similarly, if a pilot prefers to follow a different course of action, such as make a 360-degree turn for spacing to follow traffic when established in a landing or approach sequence, land on a different runway, take off from a different intersection, take off from the threshold instead of an intersection or delay his operation, *[the pilot] is expected to inform ATC accordingly.* When [requesting] a different course of action, however, the pilot is expected to cooperate so as to preclude disruption of traffic flow or creation of conflicting patterns. The pilot is also expected to use the appropriate aircraft call sign to acknowledge all ATC clearances, frequency changes, or advisory information.

(c) When weather conditions permit, during the time an IFR flight is operating, it is the direct responsibility of the pilot to avoid other aircraft since VFR flights may be operating in the same area without the knowledge of ATC. *Traffic clearances provide standard separation only between IFR flights.*

401. *AIR TRAFFIC CLEARANCE*

(a) Pilot Roles and Responsibilities

1. Acknowledge receipt and understanding of an ATC clearance.

2. *Request clarification or amendment,* as appropriate, *any time a clearance is not fully understood, or is considered unacceptable from a safety standpoint.*

3. Promptly comply with air traffic clearances upon receipt except as necessary to cope with an emergency. If deviation is necessary, advise ATC as soon as possible and obtain an amended clearance.

(b) Controller Roles and Responsibilities

1. Issue appropriate clearances for the operation to be conducted, or being conducted, in accordance with established criteria.

2. Assign altitudes in IFR clearances that are at or above the minimum IFR altitudes in controlled airspace.

3. Ensure acknowledgment by the pilot for issued information, clearance, or instructions.

4. Ensure that readbacks by the pilot of altitude, heading, or other items are correct. If incorrect, distorted, or incomplete, make corrections as appropriate.

These rules form the framework within which controllers offer clearances to pilots and may expect compliance therewith unless the pilot voices dissent. They can be summarized as follows:

1. Listen carefully to every clearance ATC gives you. If the clearance is acceptable, acknowledge the instructions and carry them out.

2. If compliance with a clearance would require you to deviate from a rule, or to do something unsafe, *inform the controller that you cannot accept the clearance, and request an amendment.*

3. You may not refuse a clearance without a sound basis for doing so (e.g., conflict with rules, safety, or inability to comply).

4. Once you accept a clearance, you must comply with it *unless an in-flight emergency requires that you do otherwise.* If you deviate from a clearance (or from any rule) under this emergency authority, *tell ATC as soon as possible and request an amended clearance.*

5. When in doubt about a controller's authority versus your own, remember FAR Section 91.3(a): You are *directly responsible for,* and are the *final authority as to,* the operation of the aircraft. Only you can bear responsibility for the safety of the flight, and only you can exercise your emergency authority when conditions warrant.

By understanding the basis of your authority as pilot in command and the authority of controllers, you also gain an understanding of how the IFR system comes together. Working with controllers is easier when you understand who is ultimately responsible for the flight.

CHAPTER 16

In Case of Emergency

Who, When, and How to Call for Help

Most pilots have heard the old saw about what to do when things go wrong in flight: In case of emergency, aviate, navigate, and communicate. This is sage advice. Controllers, flight instructors, and professional pilots agree that the single worst thing you can do when trouble strikes is to forget your primary function as a pilot: flying the airplane. True, it's important to meet problems head on, to fix what's wrong if you can. But flying is a dynamic process. You can't leave the plane to fly itself while you decide how to cope with your predicament. Too many pilots have flown straight into the ground while devoting all their attention to where they were or concentrating on completing an emergency checklist.

Unusual Attitudes

In humans, the sympathetic nervous system leaps into action when our well-being is threatened. The so-called fight-or-flight reaction is familiar to all of us. Think about the last time you were at the receiving end of a really good scare: You jumped backward, your heart pounded in your chest, you caught your breath, and you felt butterflies in your stomach. A few other physiological changes take place when you're in trouble, such as increased blood pressure, dilated pupils, heightened sensory input, and a temporary surge in physical strength. The fight-or-flight phenomenon is our primitive instinct for self-preservation at work, the first resort in the face of a perceived threat to protect our minds and bodies.

Unfortunately, this protective reaction works well only when basic physical movement—running, ducking, fighting, flailing the limbs, etc.—is called for. Flying an airplane is poorly suited to gross, uncalculated movement. The aircraft is an extension of the pilot's hands and feet, and it is only by making measured, coordinated control inputs that we can make the airplane do our bidding. For these reasons, the pilot must immediately recognize and arrest the fight-or-flight reaction in an emergency. Neither panic nor gross physical movement will get the airplane down. You have to stay in control of both yourself and the aircraft, and "do some of that pilot stuff" if you want to get home safely.

When something goes awry, it doesn't matter how serious the problem is. If you *perceive* it to be a threat to the safety of the flight and experience a fight-or-flight reaction, the first thing to do is to recognize that the uncomfortable physical sensations you're feeling are normal, and they can be controlled only by a concerted effort on your part to *calm down*.

"Yeah," some of you are saying, "that's easy to say. Try to calm down the next time you get a fire in an engine." Truth is, however, you *can* calm down if an engine catches fire. The way to control the urge to panic is to know what to do. This doesn't mean you have to memorize checklists (although you should know at least the first two or three things to do in case of life-threatening emergencies). It means you must have a *plan*. There is one plan that is *always* appropriate, in every circumstance; it will allow you to slow down your breathing and collect your thoughts. You can memorize it right now, as you read this, for there are only three steps to learn.

When faced with an emergency:

1. *Aviate:* Fly the airplane. This is Job One; it's all that matters in the final analysis. Go back to the most basic skills from your early flight instruction. If you're close to a stall, lower the nose enough to avoid it. Coordinate the rudder and the wings. Adjust power and attitude to maintain (or increase) altitude. Keep your eyes on what you're doing. If one of the aircraft's primary systems goes out, use what you have available. But whatever you do, keep flying. As soon as you quit, that's it.

2. *Navigate:* As long as you're maintaining control of the aircraft, you may as well steer it toward a safe landing area. It does no good to bail water out of a leaking boat if you're still heading out to sea, so head back to safety as quickly as possible—provided that "navigating" doesn't divert your attention from flying the aircraft.

3. *Communicate:* Inform the world at large, especially ATC, what's wrong. Set your transponder to 7700. Call for help on 121.5 (if you're already in contact

with ATC, it may be best to stay on the assigned frequency). Declare a "PAN" alert, or call "MAY-DAY." Use the word "emergency" and tell the controller your problem. If you need to land right away, get vectors to the nearest airport. Controllers can do a lot for you if they know you need help.

Once you've mastered this three-step plan, every emergency can be dealt with. When you're comfortably established flying the plane, the rest comes easily, with time in between for you to think about actually correcting the problem. After you are confident that the aircraft is under control, bring out the checklists and do what the book says; but never, ever let details distract you from the primary mission: flying. Don't get so caught up in counting the number of cranks you give the gear-extension handle that you neglect to maintain altitude. While trying to reset the main breaker, remember that you still have air-driven instruments and the wet compass when the electricity fails. If you break out of the clouds in an unusual attitude, get the wings level and put the nose on the horizon. You can mess with the fuel selectors in a minute.

Panic is the one thing you must avoid at all costs. Humans only truly panic when they don't know what to do. In the event of a catastrophic structural failure, there may really be nothing you can do. Anything less may still be an emergency but, to repeat, you can cope with almost every contingency if you: (*a*) keep flying: (*b*) head for a safe place; and (*c*) call for help.

Confess the Emergency to Yourself

The National Transportation Safety Board (NTSB) and the FAA tell us that many aircraft accidents result from the pilots' refusal (or failure) to acknowledge the fact that they are in trouble. A common initial reaction to bad news of any kind is denial. Unless a pilot realizes (and admits) that something is wrong, the condition of the aircraft or the weather may deteriorate a great deal further, reaching a point where options are limited or where remedial measures are no longer available.

No one is sure why humans consistently refuse to accept the fact that they've got serious problems. Perhaps fear makes it impossible to admit the existence of a threat. Maybe it's pride—after all, how many want to admit they're in trouble, especially if they got themselves into it? Ignorance is bliss, and if you are ignorant of the gravity of a situation you may blissfully fly right into a mountain. Whatever the reason, however, denial that you have an emergency on your hands can be fatal unless it's overcome.

Being a responsible pilot includes knowing when you need help. If a minor equipment malfunction forces you to alter your flight, you probably don't have to declare an emergency. But when you have a real-life, bona fide problem, don't kid yourself. It's sheer folly to convince yourself that it's not necessary to do anything about it. If trouble strikes, you have to know when to get busy and deal with it. ATC has an entire network available for handling emergencies and it's yours for the asking. But until you admit to yourself that you need assistance, you'll never ask anyone else for help—and what a pity it is for a pilot to die, having failed to exercise every available option.

Confess the Emergency to Others

Once you've accepted the fact that things are getting out of control, and you're prepared to keep flying the airplane as long as you're able, it's time to call in the Pros from Dover.

A pilot has the authority to declare an emergency anytime the safety of a flight is in jeopardy. As explained in chapter 15, this right includes the authority to deviate from *any* FAR under Part 91 when necessary to maintain flight safety. With this kind of wide-reaching authority in the rule book, it's puzzling why so few pilots actually make use of it.

Every ATC facility has emergency services that can be activated when an aircraft is in distress. Their radar and communications network is the finest of its kind in the world. Ground facilities have land lines to emergency personnel in almost every community. ATC specialists, working with others, can help lost aircraft get reoriented; contact police, fire, and Emergency Medical Service (EMS) units; clear other traffic from the area around an airport; guide a VFR pilot down through an unexpected cloud layer; initiate search-and-rescue missions; offer vectors to the nearest airport; talk down a panicked pilot; or provide just about any other service you may need. It's all there if you need it. The controller's radar, however, can't pick up your brain waves. If you want help, then you have to *ask*.

There is no magic formula to use when you need ATC's help. The important thing is for you to communicate enough information to enable the controller to activate the appropriate emergency services. The sooner the controller knows you're in trouble, and knows generally what the trouble is, the sooner the system can be set into motion.

The first thing you need to do is get the controller's attention and explain that you have an urgent or emergency situation on your hands. You can do this in different ways. Assuming you're already in radio contact with ATC, remain on the assigned frequency and alert the controller working your flight.* If an "urgent" (as opposed to "distress") condition exists, you should initiate your radio call with the words PAN-PAN, repeated three times. When you're in actual distress, begin by saying MAYDAY three times instead.†

If you're currently in radar contact and squawking a discrete code, do not change your transponder setting. ATC already knows where you are. If you're not receiving radar services, however, switch your transponder to Mode A, C, or S and squawk the emergency code, 7700.‡ Any ATC radar unit detecting a 7700 squawk sounds an alarm, alerting the radar operator to the presence of an aircraft in distress.

As soon as you give an alert signal (squawking an emergency code, or transmitting a PAN-PAN or MAYDAY alert), proceed to tell ATC who you are and what's wrong. When appropriate, use of the term "emergency" is impor-

* If you're not on an assigned frequency (this condition shouldn't exist during an IFR flight), tune your comm radio to 121.5 MHz. That frequency is monitored ("guarded") by every ATC ground facility, as well as by many private ground stations and commercial aircraft. A call for help on 121.5 should get you a quick response anywhere within the U.S. Airspace System.

† The ICAO defines "urgency" as a condition that causes concern about safety and the need for timely (but not immediate) assistance. An urgent condition is a *potential* distress condition. The PAN-PAN alert signals the existence of an urgent condition.

"Distress" is a condition that threatens serious and/or imminent danger to your flight. Immediate assistance is required when an aircraft is in distress. A pilot signals distress by using the MAYDAY alert.

‡ If you are ever the victim of air piracy, hijacking, or other interference by another person aboard the aircraft, squawk the "air piracy" code, 7500. If possible, call ATC and discreetly inform the controller that you are "Transponder code Seven–Five–Zero–Zero." Controllers will recognize that you are alerting them to a hijacking in progress, and will notify the proper authorities while appearing to handle your flight routinely.

tant, for when you actually declare an emergency, ATC knows you are exercising your ultimate authority as pilot in command. Include at least the following information in your initial call:

(a) The name of the station you're calling, if you know it (if you call in the blind on 121.5, any station hearing you will identify itself).

(b) Your aircraft identification and type.

(c) A brief description of the emergency. You don't have to go into great detail about your problem (not at first, anyway), but you need to generally describe your situation.

ATC will want more information as soon as you can provide it, and so will ask you for what they need. The *AIM* suggests you include as much of this as you can when you first call for help: the weather conditions where you are operating; your intentions or request; your present position and heading (or your last *known* position, if you're lost); your altitude; fuel remaining (in hours and minutes, not gallons or pounds); the number of flight crew and passengers on board; and "any other useful information."

Here is a sample radio call to an ARTCC according to the recommended formula. The aircraft is a twin turbo-prop that lost an engine in cruise flight while in radar contact with Washington Center. The condition is one of urgency, but not distress:

PAN–PAN, PAN–PAN, PAN–PAN; WASHINGTON CENTER, CHEYENNE THREE–EIGHT–NINER–KILO–BRAVO HAS AN EMERGENCY. WE HAVE SUSTAINED AN ENGINE FAILURE AND ARE UNABLE TO MAINTAIN ALTITUDE. DESCENDING THROUGH FLIGHT LEVEL TWO–THREE–

ZERO APPROXIMATELY THREE–THREE MILES
SOUTHWEST OF PATUXENT VORTAC.

The controller handling the flight will immediately alert
the appropriate ATC facilities of your location, and will
probably ask for more information:

NOVEMBER THREE–EIGHT–NINER–KILO–
BRAVO, WASHINGTON CENTER, IDENT. SAY
YOUR PRESENT HEADING AND INTENTIONS.

In this example, the aircraft should be capable of maintaining a lower altitude and is not over particularly hostile
terrain. The pilot, therefore, elects to proceed to the nearest large airport offering an ILS and full emergency facilities. The pilot has to communicate this to the controller:

CENTER, NINER–KILO–BRAVO IS PRESENTLY
ON A HEADING OF ONE–EIGHT–ZERO. WE
NEED A CLEARANCE TO A LOWER ALTITUDE
AND VECTORS TO RICHMOND/BYRD FIELD
FOR LANDING.

The ARTCC should be able to handle all the requested
details, and provide vectors for the Cheyenne to land at
RIC. In these two short radio calls, the pilot has alerted
ATC to the need for help, explained the situation, and
made clear what sort of help is needed. As the aircraft
nears the destination, the controller will alert emergency
facilities at RIC and coordinate the clearing of traffic from
the area to enable the Cheyenne to make the shortest possible approach. ATC may also gather additional information about the flight (such as fuel remaining or number of
persons on board), and can provide up-to-the-minute
weather advisories for the route to the airport.

Sometimes, the nature of an emergency only allows a

pilot to make a single call for help before the radios fail or must be shut down. An onboard fire, for instance, may require the pilot to disconnect all electrical systems, including the transponder and the radios, as quickly as possible. In this situation, there may only be enough time to transmit a quick "MAYDAY." The pilot doesn't have the luxury of carrying on a conversation (or even waiting for an answer, in some cases). When a crisis like this arises, then, your first radio call had better be good. Include as much of the information mentioned above as you can, and provide any other information that will help a search-and-rescue effort locate you, such as color of aircraft, whether you have manually activated your Emergency Locator Transmitter, whether there is emergency equipment aboard, and any major landmarks you can see from the cockpit.

If all of this sounds to you like an awful lot of information to remember for one single radio call, that's because it is. But it's not that hard to remember. When you're forced to make a distress call and you know you don't have time to establish definite radio contact (much less play Twenty Questions with a controller), just remember this: If you call on 121.5, someone should hear you. If you squawk 7700, someone should see you, even if it's for only a minute. When you make the call, tell your would-be rescuers *everything you can think of* that will help them locate you after you come down.

Here is a sample distress call from the pilot of a single-engine airplane that is neither in radio nor radar contact with ATC. There is smoke in the cockpit, and the pilot must make a quick broadcast and then shut off the master switch:

MAYDAY MAYDAY MAYDAY, ANY STATION,
MOONEY THREE–EIGHT–NINER–KILO–BRAVO

HAS A FIRE ONBOARD. SQUAWKING SEVEN–
SEVEN–ZERO–ZERO, APPROXIMATELY TWO–
ZERO MILES SOUTHEAST OF SALINA VORTAC
AT NINER THOUSAND, DESCENDING FOR AN
OFF-AIRPORT LANDING. TWO PERSONS ON
BOARD; AIRCRAFT IS WHITE; ELT IS ACTI-
VATED. SHUTTING DOWN ALL ELECTRICAL
SYSTEMS AT THIS TIME. REPEAT, MAYDAY
MAYDAY MAYDAY, MOONEY THREE–EIGHT–
NINER–KILO–BRAVO ON FIRE, TWO–ZERO
SOUTHEAST OF SALINA DESCENDING OUT OF
NINER THOUSAND FOR EMERGENCY LANDING.

This entire radio call should take less than thirty seconds, especially since adrenaline tends to make one speak
faster than normal. Not every distress call will be this complete, but you get the idea—give as much information as
you can in as short a time as possible.

Snap, Crackle, Pop

It's rare when modern comm radios fail. It's even rarer for
both radios to fail in the same flight. Factor in the odds
against both comm radios going south on you during an
IFR flight while you're in the clouds, and it seems almost
impossible that you'd ever need to know the rules for failed
communications during IFR flight. But the sad fact is,
comm failures happen. There are certain weak links in the
radio chain that are less reliable than modern electronics.
All your radios require a power source; you could lose
your alternator or even a main power buss. In most installations, both comm radios use the same VHF antenna; if
the antenna or connecting lead fail, there go the radios.
The cabin speaker, the headphone jack, your micro-

phones, the audio amplifier, the push-to-talk switch, and a dozen fuses or circuit breakers are all elements that can fail—and take your communications capability with them. Many seasoned pilots have learned the value of carrying a hand-held, battery-powered portable comm or nav/comm radio. Besides being handy for copying ATIS and clearances without running down the aircraft's battery, it can save your skin if the main radios fold.

This book is based entirely upon the premise that two-way radio communication is the bond that holds the IFR system together. When you lose the ability to talk to (or hear) ATC, the very nature of IFR flight is altered. You have only one goal, and that is to complete the flight safely according to a prearranged contingency plan: the FAA's procedures for failed communications. Under these rules, a communications failure is defined as any loss of ability to *transmit or receive* voice communication with ATC. When such a failure occurs, ATC doesn't have any way to control your progress. They must be able to predict what path you will take, what altitude you will fly, and how far you will go, if they are to maintain separation between you and other aircraft (especially when you arrive at a busy area for landing). The only way ATC can predict what you will do is through the specific rules governing IFR flight without two-way communications. Unless controllers can rely on you to follow those rules, they will be forced to clear *all* traffic from an entire area while waiting and watching to see what you'll do next, resulting in massive delays and, in effect, a total shutdown of the IFR system in that area.

The rules for getting down safely without communications ability are reasonably simple, although at first glance they seem disjointed. They can be found in chapter 5, section 4 of the *AIM,* "Two-Way Radio Communications

Failure." Every pilot should read and study the entire text of this section.

Basically, there are three rules to remember for failed communications:

1. If you're in VFR conditions when the radio failure strikes, or if you break out of the clouds into VFR conditions (where you can see the ground, that is), *maintain VFR,* land as soon as practicable, and then contact ATC to let them know where you are and what happened.

2. If you're in IFR conditions when you lose the radios, fly according to the *route, altitude,* and *clearance limit* restrictions set forth in the FARs (discussed on pp. 188–193). Consider separately *what route* you'll fly, *how high,* and *how far* you'll go before you shoot an approach and try to land.

3. If your transponder is still working (that is, if you still have power), squawk 7700 for one minute (to get ATC's attention), then change the squawk to 7600 (to tell ATC exactly what the trouble is—lost communications) for fifteen minutes. Repeat this sixteen-minute cycle continuously until you land or until radio communications are reestablished.

If, when the radio go out, you are in VFR conditions above a cloud deck (meaning you'll have to go into the soup to land), keep flying the IFR clearance. It's better to follow the "lost comm" rules (and end up where ATC expects you to end up) than to descend blindly into clouds and arrive, IFR, at an airport where no one expects you.

If, instead, the failure occurs while you're in VFR conditions with clear air below, and you determine that you can maintain VFR and land without going IFR, the safest thing to do is to start acting like a VFR pilot: Go to a VFR altitude (even or odd thousands, plus 500 feet), squawk 1200, watch carefully for other traffic, and get to an airfield using pilotage skills and VFR sectionals. ATC also recommends that, in order to avoid climbing or descending into IFR traffic, you turn perpendicular to your course line until you are well clear of the airway, then change to an appropriate VFR altitude.

The route, altitude,* and clearance limit rules are governed primarily by common sense. Depending upon how complete your last clearance was, you may be able to proceed directly to your destination (maintaining one altitude along the way) and shoot the approach when you get there. In crowded conditions, however, controllers are often unable to clear you all the way to your destination. In that case, you will have received clearance limits and "expect further clearance at . . ." instructions. All these are factors in determining how far you go, and when.

Route Rules: As for *what path* you should take when your radios quit, the FARs say you should fly one of the following routes, as best fits your situation:

(a) *If a specific route was assigned to your flight* in an ATC clearance, fly that route (use the last assigned route, if you were given an updated or amended clearance).

Or:

(b) *If you're being vectored to some fix,* go directly to that fix and *then* proceed on the last route assigned.

---

* In this chapter, "altitude" is used interchangeably with "flight level," when appropriate (when an aircraft is flying at or above 18,000 feet msl).

Or:

(c) *If no route has yet been assigned,* fly the route you were
told to *expect* in a further clearance.

Or:

(d) *If no route has yet been assigned, and you weren't given a
route to expect,* fly the route you filed in your instrument flight plan (aren't you glad you wrote it down
on your communications log?).

These rules can be made to fit virtually any situation and
should help you figure out the appropriate route under
most circumstances. The main "route rule" to remember
is: Go where ATC told you; if they didn't tell you where to
go, follow your flight plan.

Altitude Rules: Altitude rules seem to cause the most confusion, and that's understandable. But the altitude rules
are easier to follow when you consider they have one basic
function: keeping you from meeting the ground until you
intend to do so. ATC would rather have you fly a little too
high than a little too low. Consequently, you are supposed
to maintain the *highest* appropriate altitude for each route
segment.* By looking at your clearance and the Minimum
En route Altitudes (MEAs) shown on IFR en route charts,
you can always determine the appropriate altitude to fly.

---

* A "route segment" is a portion of your route that has a distinct
beginning and end. For example, when flying a Victor airway, you
ordinarily cross several intersections or VORs. Each intersection or
VOR marks the end of one route segment and the beginning of the
next. Whenever the MEA changes, you must recalculate the proper
altitude to fly. If there is a Minimum Crossing Altitude (MCA) for a
particular fix, you must be at or above that altitude when crossing that
point.

The FAA says that for a given route segment you are to maintain the *highest* of these three altitudes:

(a)　The altitude last *assigned* to you

(b)　The MEA for the segment

Or:

(c)　The altitude you were told to *expect* in a further clearance, if any

"What? Huh? When do I know which one to fly?" That's a common reaction when pilots read those three choices. But the answer is right above the rules: *Always pick the highest of the three.*

In actual practice, following altitude rules is pretty easy. As mentioned above, the first priority is staying off the ground; so, when in doubt, take the higher altitude. To determine the right altitude for a given route segment, follow these steps:

1. Stick to your Last Assigned Altitude (LAA) whenever possible. Circle it on the communications log. Set it into your altitude alerter. Keep it foremost in your mind, for although MEAs come and go during a flight, you return to the LAA whenever it's the higher of the two. Nine flights out of ten, in fact, you will find yourself cruising at an LAA far above the MEA along the entire route. In that situation, the LAA is all you have to remember until you set up for the approach.

2. Look at the MEA along each segment of your route. Any time the MEA is *higher* than the LAA, climb to that MEA *for that segment only.* As soon as the MEA drops back down to (or below) the LAA, return to

the LAA upon reaching the next route segment.*

3. If you were told to "expect" a higher altitude "in ten minutes" (most often heard in departure clearances) or "after crossing XYZ intersection," the "expected" altitude becomes your new assigned altitude (your new LAA) when you reach the ten-minute mark (or the XYZ intersection). Be careful, however. If the "expected" altitude is *lower* than the LAA, maintain the LAA until you are ready to begin the approach.

Clearance Limit Rules: Clearance limit rules, like route rules, are pretty straightforward. After you decide which route you're going to follow, you can determine the proper altitude for each segment. As you continue toward your destination (or the clearance limit), it's time to start thinking about how you're going to get down.

Rule One says you're supposed to go all the way to the clearance limit if communications are lost. Except for those occasions when you fly into an extremely busy terminal area, most initial clearances will have no intermediate clearance limit—you're cleared all the way to the destination. That's a nice clearance to have if the radios go out, because in that case Rule One lets you go all the way to the destination airport.

The rules for moving *beyond* clearance limits are the ones

---

* By the way, unless there is a Minimum Crossing Altitude (MCA) for a particular intersection or navaid, don't begin climbing to the new MEA until you actually begin the new segment. The FAA builds in enough clearance for you to climb from one MEA to the next at a modest climb gradient (a maximum of 150 feet/nm) without risking a collision with terrain. If there are areas where terrain requires you to cross a fix at or above a certain altitude, the chart will list a MCA. Obviously, you must climb to the MCA before reaching a fix that has one.

you need to stop and think about. They are "what and when" rules; they specify when you can go beyond the limit, and what to do from there. As you might expect, you have to watch the clock and depart a clearance limit only at the appropriate time.

Two different *times* apply to the "what and when" rules. They are the Expect Further Clearance, or EFC, time (usually given by the controller along with the clearance limit), and your ETA. ATC will have your current ETA if you've been giving position reports. Otherwise, calculate an approximate ETA by adding the "time en route" as filed in your flight plan to the time you actually departed.

There are two "what and when" rules, but only one applies to your flight, depending upon whether the clearance limit is a fix from which an instrument approach procedure begins.* The rules are as follows:

VERY ——
IMPORTANT !!!

1. When the clearance limit *is* a fix from which an approach to your destination begins:

   (a) *What:*   Begin the descent or descent and approach.

   (b) *When:*   At the EFC time (if you received one) or at the ETA.

2. If the clearance limit *is not* a fix from which an approach begins:

   (a) *What:*   Leave the clearance limit and proceed to a fix along your route from which an approach *does* begin.

* Typically, a given approach procedure can begin at any one of several fixes, such as : A feeder VOR, an intersection, a compass locator/marker, the airport itself, or an NDB on the airfield. When such a fix applies to a given approach, it will be indicated on the approach plate as an initial approach fix.

(b) *When:*   At the EFC time (if you received one) or *as soon as you arrive* at the clearance limit.

(c) *And then:*   Upon reaching the fix from which an approach begins, commence the approach at the ETA.

If you arrive at any of the above-described fixes *after* your EFC time or ETA, proceed directly to the next step in the plan. Accordingly, if you reach an initial approach fix *after* your original ETA, commence the approach procedure immediately.

As for the question of *which* approach to use, that's strictly a matter of pilot discretion. When an aircraft loses radio capability, all approaches to the airport are held open during a thirty-minute "arrival window."* If you know what approaches are in use (if you were able to copy the ATIS before the radio broke), shoot that approach if your equipment permits. Common sense suggests you should take advantage of the most precise approach available. If there is an ILS to a long runway, that's probably safer than a circling NDB approach. You take what you can get, however, and if your nav/comm radios are out of commission, the NDB may be all you have left.

When flying any instrument approach, pilots like to know what's going on down below. It's important to know the sky and wind conditions, whether other traffic is operating, the altimeter setting, and which approaches or runways are in use. You, unfortunately, are operating without communications capability, so neither ATIS nor Unicom are available. This brings up an important issue to keep in mind when you begin the approach: You *must* be

---

* You can see, therefore, why it's important to arrive at the destination airport as close as possible to the ETA; that's when ATC expects you to be there.

ready to circle-to-land, and you should shoot the approach to the highest minimums on the chart. Several factors contribute to this recommendation:

1. The last altimeter setting you received may be hours old. If the setting in the Kollsman window is off by more than a few one-hundredths of an inch, a descent to the MDA could be a descent into terrain.

2. Until you get close to the ground, you won't have any idea of the prevailing winds on the airfield. We are taught to land upwind for a reason: crosswind and downwind landings aren't as safe as landing into the wind. You will have to circle the airfield and get a look at a wind sock, tee, or tetrahedron before you can make an informed choice of runways.

3. If your destination is a controlled field, you must wait for a light gun signal to land (a steady green light). When you come sliding down the ILS and break out of the clouds lined up to land, complete the approach *only* after the tower gives you permission to do so. Accordingly, you must be ready to break off the descent and circle if you receive any light signal other than steady green (or if you receive none at all).

Maybe It's Broke, Maybe It Ain't

Unless your communications failure is the result of something conclusive—a complete failure of the electrical system, for instance—you may be suffering from what *seems* like a total loss of communications ability, but what is, in fact, only a partial breakdown. Aside from the obvious "dumb" causes of temporary radio silence (sitting on the microphone switch, volume turned down, squelch too high, headset unplugged, a popped circuit breaker), your problem could be a "half" failure. Maybe the receiver is broken, but ATC can still hear you. On the other hand, maybe you're receiving okay, but no one hears you when you transmit.

At one time or another, virtually all of us have experienced that fleeting moment of terror when, after flying straight and level for a while (usually at night), you realize that *you don't hear anyone on the radio,* and haven't for several minutes. "Uh oh," you mumble quietly, "what if the radio's gone out?" Ordinarily, about the time you get really concerned, you hear some pilot or controller transmit something. Soon your blood pressure ebbs and you settle back into your seat.

If you've experienced this phenomenon often enough, you may have reached a point where you no longer worry if an en route frequency is quiet for a long time. A true communications failure may thus go undiscovered for quite a while, especially if temporary silence is a normal occurrence in that area.*

If you begin to suspect you've lost your comm radios, check it out. Call ATC and see if you get a response. Call several times, in case the controller hears you but is busy with another aircraft. Turn the squelch all the way down and see if you hear static—or anything at all—on the frequency. Make sure that the volume is turned up (and that the power didn't somehow get turned off—a common occurrence when changing frequencies in rough air). Switch to your other comm radio. (You don't fly IFR with just one comm, do you? I don't care if it *is* legal, it's not smart.) Change from headsets to the cabin speaker. Bypass the

* Silence may be normal during light traffic hours or in the en route phase of your flight. In a busy ARSA or TCA, however, silence of more than a few seconds is unusual. A hush of more than a minute should prompt you to call ATC to see if they hear you (or you them).

intercom (if you have one). Jiggle headphone and microphone plugs. Try a backup microphone. Look for tripped
circuit breakers or fuses. Did the avionics master switch get
turned off? Swap headsets with a passenger. Try a different frequency, starting with the previous ATC frequency
assigned to you. Consult a VFR sectional and tune in a
local airport frequency. Try calling on 121.5, if no other
frequency yields results.

If the problem persists, connect the nav radio "voice"
output to the speaker or headsets, and see if you can still
pick up a navaid identifier. If so, you may be in luck; ATC
can transmit over the voice channel of many VORs and
VORTACs. As soon as they realize you're not receiving on
the comm frequencies, a controller or FSS specialist may
try to call you, using a nearby navaid.

If nothing helps and you just can't seem to raise a
voice on any comm channel or navaid, don't give up. As
long as you have power available to the comm radios,
you *may* still be transmitting okay (and ATC may be receiving you just fine). To allow for that possibility, conduct your flight according to the "lost communication"
rules (be sure to use the 7700/7600 squawk sequence),
but *announce what you're doing* on 121.5 MHz as you go.
For example, if you climb in order to conform to a higher
MEA, call and identify yourself, give your location, and
announce "now climbing from Niner Thousand to new
MEA One–Three Thousand." Make periodic position reports, even if your transponder "reply" light indicates
you're being followed on radar. When you arrive at your
destination and commence an approach procedure, announce *which* approach you're flying. If you break out
of the murk and make visual contact with the tower, use
the tower frequency (or 121.5) and ask for light signals. In
this way, you can actually maintain partial communi-

cations with ATC, and they know what you're up to every step of the way.

If you experience a "partial" failure of the opposite type—that is, you *receive* fine, but no one seems to hear you—you're in much better shape. All you have to do is inform ATC that you've lost transmit capability. The controllers can steer you around, asking you to squawk certain codes (or ident or whatever), to acknowledge an instruction or answer a yes or no question.

Alerting the controller that you've got a communications problem is easy if your transponder is working; but what if some power surge or broken solder connection costs you both your transmit capability *and* your transponder? This is a more serious situation, but it's still manageable if you follow the route, altitude, and clearance limit rules above. When your transponder goes, you will most likely drop completely off ATC's radar. Except in terminal areas (where radar is designed to pick up any airborne traffic regardless of transponder status), the radar system won't detect an aircraft without a transponder return.

In any case, the controller handling your flight will certainly notice the loss of your transponder return (whether your bare radar return shows up or not). The controller's first reaction will be to alert you that radar contact is lost. If you don't acknowledge that call, it will be repeated. After a few unsuccessful attempts to make contact, the controller knows you've lost communications ability.

If a primary target is still visible on the radar screen, a controller can establish communications by asking you to fly a certain vector for a few seconds. If you respond (if the radar target turns to comply with the request), communications are reestablished and ATC can still control your progress.

If you drop completely off radar, however, ATC has no

way to know if you are even still airborne, much less whether you're receiving their transmissions. Still, you should monitor the appropriate frequency for each sector or area you pass through in case ATC has instructions for you (it's a good idea to monitor 121.5 on the other comm radio, should that be the frequency ATC uses to talk to you). They may have to wait until you reach a terminal area to pick you up on radar again.

When approaching an airport for landing, monitor the tower frequency. As soon as you can see the tower, listen for instructions and watch for light gun signals. If it's daylight, acknowledge radio or light signals by rocking the wings or waggling the rudder (take it easy with the rudder when flying low and slow). At night, acknowledge instructions by flashing your landing or navigation lights.

Bringing It All Together

The rules of emergency management are pretty simple. Fly the aircraft, head for safety, and communicate the problem. In case two-way communications are lost, you may still be able to communicate "one-way." Regardless, you have a plan to follow: You know what route to fly, you know what altitude(s) to select, and you know when and where to go for landing. The loss of radio communications is a serious problem and it's disconcerting at best. It is, however, completely survivable if you take a deep breath, calm down, and follow the FAA's plan.

Case Study: Failure to Declare an Emergency

As this book was in the final stages of revision, a major air carrier disaster near New York's John F. Kennedy Airport (JFK) brought into vivid focus the importance of complete, accurate communications when trouble strikes. A study of this accident reveals numerous communications errors that eventually doomed the flight, and offers valuable lessons to every pilot who gets caught in an urgent or distress situation.

It cannot be said too often: If you have, or even *think* you have, an urgent situation on board, declare a PAN-PAN alert and explain the situation *in detail* to the controller. If you have an emergency situation on your hands, declare an emergency. Begin your transmission by stating "MAYDAY-MAYDAY-MAYDAY." Use the word "emergency" in your radio call. Describe the problem in as much detail as possible *as quickly as possible.* If you're in trouble, yet fail to call ATC and make the nature of the problem perfectly clear, then you will almost certainly fall victim to the worst kind of communications failure—one that costs lives.

On January 25, 1990, the flight crew of a Boeing 707 allowed a fuel problem to develop on a flight to New York City. They also believed they had communicated their predicament to ATC. But on that stormy night over Long Island, Avianca Flight 52 never received emergency handling for one simple reason: the flight crew never asked for it.*

History of the Flight: Flight 52 flew from Bogota and Medellin, Colombia, to JFK with 142 passengers and nine

---

* The information detailed here is based on news reports and interviews available when this book went to press. As of this writing, the NTSB had published no official reports or findings concerning the probable cause or causes of this crash. When those reports are issued, the conclusions expressed here may be found inaccurate. The author makes no attempt to judge or determine conclusively the ability or capacity of any person, living or dead, or of any particular type of aircraft or equipment.

crew members on board. Due to weather and traffic delays in the New York area, the crew was ordered to hold three times as the flight progressed northward along the eastern seaboard. These three holds apparently added between eighty-five and ninety minutes to the total flight time. By the time the aircraft was in the domain of New York Center, the pilot apparently knew that the plane's fuel reserves were low. At the captain's request, the copilot related this situation to controllers at the ARTCC, but for some reason failed to properly explain the flight's status or declare an emergency. Instead, according to ATC tapes, the copilot told Center, "We need a priority. We're low on fuel." He also told Center they were too low on fuel to proceed to Boston (their alternate destination), some forty minutes away.

The airplane was vectored for the ILS Runway 22 Left approach in stormy, windy conditions. At about 9:24 P.M. local time, the crew executed a missed approach and asked for another attempt at the ILS. Flight 52 crashed ten minutes later while being vectored for the second approach. The 707 went down in a wooded neighborhood on Long Island, just inland from Long Island Sound. Of the 151 people on board, 78 survived. That there was no post-crash fire is probably what prevented the death toll from going much higher. But it is also the absence of a fire—combined with reports from investigators that none of the engines appeared to be developing power at impact—that suggests the crash resulted from a frighteningly simple cause: the aircraft ran out of fuel.

Communicating an Emergency: That an airliner can run out of fuel is surprising in and of itself. All flights operating in U.S. airspace are required to carry certain minimum fuel reserves, and the requirements for air carriers—especially international flights—are particularly strict.

Given the reputed unreliability of fuel quantity gauges in some aircraft, pilots are taught to put their faith in power setting charts, fuel consumption tables, and the clock when computing fuel range.* But, regardless of how they managed to arrive in the New York area with so little fuel remaining, why didn't the crew request emergency handling?

The *AIM* specifically provides a communications guideline for a low-fuel condition. It advises pilots that if the remaining usable fuel aboard the aircraft suggests the need for immediate handling upon reaching the destination, the pilot should advise ATC that the aircraft has reached minimum-fuel status. By definition, this advisory is not a declaration of an emergency, but it does alert controllers that an emergency situation is possible if any delay occurs. In addition, when ATC receives a minimum-fuel advisory from an aircraft, that status is relayed to succeeding controllers as the flight is handed off.

The *AIM* further dictates that, should the situation deteriorate to a point that demands traffic priority to ensure a safe landing, the pilot should (*a*) *declare an emergency,* (*b*) account low fuel, and (*c*) report the amount of fuel remaining *in minutes.*

It's clear, then, that the crew had several techniques available to alert controllers that the flight needed help urgently. They could have:

- advised ATC of "minimum-fuel status";
- said the flight was in "distress" (an ICAO term);

---

* Some early reports from the investigation suggest that the 707's fuel gauges indicated that sufficient fuel remained for the second landing attempt. If true, this further underscores the need for careful fuel monitoring—the crew should have suspected that the gauges were giving a reading inconsistent with their fuel calculations.

- repeated "MAYDAY" three times and asked for immediate help;
- set the Boeing's transponder to squawk 7700; or
- told controllers, "Flight 52 is declaring an emergency."

The crew did none of these things.

Why the Misunderstanding? The Avianca crew's radio calls to New York Center failed to adequately inform controllers of the flight's predicament for at least three reasons. In the first place, the crew asked for a "priority." "Priority" is not an approved term for pilot-controller communications. Just what did "priority" mean to the pilot? To the controllers? The word isn't the same as "emergency," and so is open to any interpretation the listener assigns to it. After the pilot asked for a "priority," ATC released the flight from its third hold ahead of schedule. In doing so, the controllers apparently thought they had complied with the pilot's wishes. In short, by merely asking for "priority" without giving more information, the pilot committed the first communications error.

Furthermore, the copilot didn't say how serious the fuel condition on board was. He didn't tell controllers how many *minutes* of fuel remained as the *AIM* advises. Instead, he just said the plane was "low on fuel." How low is "low"? Were they too low on fuel for a missed approach? Apparently, fuel was low enough that the crew could have declared an emergency, but they did not do so. Again, the controllers had no way of knowing the situation facing the flight. The crew's ambiguous use of "low" to describe their fuel condition, therefore, was the second communications error.

The third problem with what the crew told New York Center was that they reported they didn't have enough fuel on board to reach their alternate. This is important information, to be sure, but *it wasn't enough*. Even if the controllers knew that Boston was a forty-minute flight for a Boeing 707, the only message the crew managed to communicate to ATC was, "We have something less than forty minutes' worth of fuel remaining." But *how much* less than forty minutes? Did they still have, for example, enough fuel on board to last thirty-five minutes? Did they have less than five minutes' worth? Again, the controllers weren't fully informed, and so didn't know the situation.

There are conflicting reports as to whether the Avianca flight crew's messages about the fuel problem were relayed from New York Center to the TRACON when Flight 52 was handed off to New York Approach. Still, given that none of the earlier transmissions was a declaration of an emergency, a minimum-fuel advisory, or even an obvious request for help, it's not clear whether the information even *should* have been relayed between controllers.

The Final Error: One last communications error may have occurred when the crew flew the missed approach. According to preliminary reports, the airplane descended below the glideslope on the ILS (at one point, the cockpit voice recorder apparently picked up alert signals from the Ground Proximity Warning System [GPWS] and/or the stall warning system). The approach seemed lost, so the crew (wisely) decided to execute a missed approach and try again. But here they apparently erred again when JFK tower handed them off to Approach. After the handoff, the copilot again mentioned "low fuel," but still didn't declare an emergency. The controller working the flight informed the pilots that he intended to take the aircraft out over Long Island Sound and back around for the ILS. When asked if that was acceptable, the copilot reportedly replied "Okay."

Consider this scenario for a moment: here was an aircraft critically low on fuel, yet the pilots apparently accepted a clearance to fly almost *twenty-five miles* northeast of JFK and get in line for another approach. If reports to this effect prove correct, then the accepted clearance was certainly the final straw, any prior miscommunication notwithstanding. The flight crew declared a missed approach and executed the go-around at about 9:24 P.M. local time, then dropped off radar at 9:34 P.M. In other words, even after all the prior delays and the missed approach, *there was still enough fuel on board to last ten minutes.* Had the pilots declared an emergency even as late as the beginning of the go-around, the approach controller could almost certainly have brought the flight around for another ILS within that time.

That any person should die aboard an aircraft is a sad reality. That this loss may have resulted from miscommunication between the flight crew and ATC is the worst kind of tragedy.

The primary lesson we can learn from the fate of Avianca Flight 52 is simple: confess an emergency to ATC *early* and *completely.* When you think you're in trouble, there is no time to be shy. If you're wrong about the emergency, and your call for help was unnecessary, then you may have to fill out a form or two for the FAA. But if you're right, quick action (and a quick call for help) could avert disaster.

Earlier Signs of Trouble: This account offers one other communications lesson that may be less than obvious. There was a breakdown in communications between pilot and controller much *earlier* than 9:24 P.M. New York time. This first mistake occurred during the en route portion of Flight 52, when the pilot accepted three different holds that eventually exhausted all of the plane's fuel reserves.

As detailed in chapter 15, a pilot is obligated to refuse *any* clearance that requires a rule violation, places the flight in jeopardy, or is beyond the capabilities of pilot or aircraft. You learned in your basic instrument training that a proper hold clearance always includes an "Expect Further Clearance" (EFC) time. In fact, pilots are taught to refuse any hold instruction lacking such a parameter. In other words, any time you're told to enter a holding pattern, you have some idea how long the hold should last. That time may vary, of course—the hold may later be cut short or extended—but you have at least an *estimate* at the outset.

With this in mind, we must assume that the Avianca pilot received an EFC time with each of the three holds ATC issued. If the crew kept up with fuel-consumption rates during the flight as they should have, they would have known fuel was getting short when the second or third hold was issued. The flight was required to carry enough fuel to reach JFK, then proceed to Boston, and still remain aloft for another forty-five minutes at normal cruising speed. After the forty-five minute reserve was used up in the first holding patterns, the pilot was obligated to either refuse further holding, advise ATC of minimum-fuel status, or request a diversion to a closer airport for refueling. By accepting the three successive holds and allowing some ninety minutes' fuel to be burned, the pilot may have sealed Flight 52's fate long before its arrival in New York Center's airspace.

Further developments continue in the wake of the Avianca crash. On February 21, 1990, the NTSB called upon Federal Aviation Administrator James Busey to urge all domestic and foreign air carriers to remind pilots of the importance of thorough knowledge of "flight operating and traffic control rules and procedures, including standard phraseology." That, fellow pilots, is the point repeatedly stressed in this book.

In the IFR context, clear communications are always vital. But in the event of a threatened or real emergency, proper communications may be your only chance for survival. In the aftermath of Flight 52, that lesson becomes uncomfortably clear.

Epilogue: On March 27, 1990, the NTSB released transcripts of the cockpit voice recorder from Flight 52. Ironically, it appears that the crew members fell victim to miscommunication among themselves. The flight crew, conversing in Spanish, apparently discussed the fact that they were "in an emergency." Twice within the final minutes of the flight, the captain ordered the first officer to "Advise [the controller] that we are in an emergency." The first officer acknowledged the command, and *later confirmed to the captain that he had informed ATC of the emergency.* Yet the record is clear—the first officer repeatedly used terms like "priority" and "low" fuel, but he never declared an *emergency.* The captain, first officer, and flight engineer all assumed that ATC knew what their situation was. That assumption seems to be what eventually downed Flight 52.

CHAPTER 17

Tales of Woe and Intrigue

True Stories of Miscommunication

The Two-Way Street

Throughout this book, you've been challenged to think ahead when talking on the radio. You've learned to concentrate on whom you're calling, why you're calling them, and what you're going to say, all *before* you hit the push-to-talk button and go on the air. But radio signals travel not only *from* your radio to the ears of others, they also travel *to* you from ATC and other pilots. For at least half of the time, therefore, you are responding to radio calls instead of initiating them. In those situations, your job is to listen to the call, try to understand it, and respond to it by word or action.

You may be the type who takes every step you can to make your outgoing radio communications the clearest in the skies. You may buy the newest radios and headsets, speak clearly and slowly, use appropriate terminology, and make pithy, information-packed radio calls that would make any senior controller proud. But no matter how good you are at talking, you've got to be equally good at listening or you're only half a communicator.

The point is this: Radio communication requires both give-and-take. You transmit information, and ATC receives it. If a controller issues a vector, you acknowledge it and turn the aircraft. Being a good IFR communicator means assisting with the constant, smooth flow of information *in both directions*. It's what this book is all about.

Keeping the Lines Open

So what can you do to help keep information moving efficiently in both directions? Proper radio technique is the starting point, but technique alone won't solve the problem if you're caught out in the cold by someone else's mistake. What happens when "the other pilot" steps on your transmission, preventing ATC from hearing your request? What do you do if you are cleared to "execute the approach," but you don't know which one? Who is to blame when the tower controller clears you to land, but on the wrong runway? What if you go ahead and land on the *right* runway? What will you do if there is a communications mixup between ATC and some other aircraft? Will you just keep making correct radio calls and hope the misunderstandings of others straighten themselves out?

The solution is for you to become a problem-solver. I know, your hands are already full flying the airplane, right? Well, the pilot's first responsibility is safety, and one of the ways to maintain the highest safety margin possible is to identify and correct errors in communication, regardless of who is at fault.

A Problem-Solving Approach

Analyzing and solving problems is the essence of this chapter. What follows herein is a short collection of "war stories," anecdotes, and documented mishaps. All are true, and all illustrate how easy it is for simple errors in diction, grammar, or numbers to degenerate into major safety hazards (or worse). All aircraft tail numbers, and most of the locations, have been changed to protect the easily embarrassed. In each example, we learn a lesson by evaluating what actually happened, as well as what *could* have happened if corrections had not been quickly applied. By studying case histories in this way, we strive to avoid similar experiences, and we prepare to deal with them when they arise (as they inevitably do).

All of these accounts vary widely in both cause and effect, but they all share one insidious factor: In every case, someone was told one thing, but *thought* they heard another. In other words, they *assumed* they knew what was said—but they were wrong. Perhaps a pilot heard only part of a transmission and guessed at the rest. Maybe someone on the ground heard a pilot say something that seemed obviously wrong, so the controller assumed he knew what the pilot *meant* to say (and ignored the actual message).

Whatever the facts surrounding an IFR communications mixup, the risk is always grave. A pilot may follow an incorrect vector, descend to the wrong altitude, fly an approach straight into a mountain, or even collide with another aircraft as a result of a breach in the radio link.

The Risks of Relaxation

Not even the finest pilots or the most experienced controllers can operate safely if they don't share information accurately and continuously. In many cases, communication errors afflict the *most* skilled pilots and controllers. This is contrary to what you might expect (the obvious conclusion being that experience leads to skill, and skill prevents mistakes), but it is also true. Why are the experts plagued by simple blunders the same as the rest of us?

The culprit seems to be found in the way human animals acquire new skills. We tend to develop routines and master repetitive tasks on a subconscious level. As a result, complacency sometimes replaces concentration when a person performs the same tasks (e.g., flies the same approaches and talks to the same controllers) time and time again. Complacency, manifesting itself as a high pilot "comfort" level, will allow your mind to wander and your concentration to relax. One consequence of this lapse may be inattention to detail, resulting in a type of "cognitive illusion," in which your ears receive certain input, but your mind *perceives* it differently; in short, you hear what you *expect* to hear instead of what *actually* reached your ears.

A Common Problem

In reviewing the situations described in this chapter, you will spot numerous situations in which "hearing what they expected to hear" caused pilots and controllers alike to make seemingly innocuous mistakes—but mistakes which had the potential to bring about disaster.

You are invited to analyze each scenario, placing yourself in the position of each pilot and/or controller. Applying the lessons of earlier chapters, review the actions of every person concerned with a critical eye. Did they use proper radio technique? Did they make assumptions? How would you have reacted in the same situation? What could you have done to prevent or correct the problem before things got out of hand?

A Common Solution

You may find yourself consistently arriving at one conclusion in your analyses: In almost every instance, a simple question would have fixed everything. The act of *asking* for a transmission to be repeated, or for an explanation, would have prevented any misunderstanding and averted any conflict. In many of the examples, as you will see, someone did ask for a clarification, thereby resolving the matter without incident.

If you remember only one thing from this chapter, remember this: The single most important step the pilot can take to ensure clear and accurate communications is to *verify* everything. If you receive an instruction that is clearly wrong, if it appears someone else misunderstood something you said, if something just doesn't "feel right," *ask*. Ask them to "say again." Repeat back what you thought you heard and ask if you heard it correctly. If you heard it right but it doesn't make sense, *ask for an explanation*. The worst communications error is to *assume* you know what someone means. Making assumptions is rarely wise; it is sheer folly to do so when the safety of your flight hangs in the balance. The prudent pilot would no more "assume" what another is thinking than "assume" there is fuel in the tanks before takeoff. By making it your policy to read back, verify, and clarify every altitude, vector, and clearance, you become a safe, thorough IFR communicator.

True Stories

Right Airport, Wrong Approach: The following situation involved a controller misstating the obvious, and illustrates the risks posed if a pilot decides not to point out an obvi-

ous error. On a cloudy, bumpy afternoon, an A–36 Bonanza was en route into the Dallas area from the southeast.
The Bonanza was in radar contact with Approach Control
and was being vectored into position for an approach to
Addison Airport, a controlled field a few miles north of
Love Field. The only runway at Addison is 7,200-foot Runway 15–33. A stiff wind was pushing low ceilings and thunderstorms into the area from the northwest, and many
aircraft near the storm front and in the DFW Airport vicinity were diverting around large buildups. Consequently, the area controllers were extremely busy, as
normal traffic flow was disrupted.

The current ATIS indicated dropping ceilings and gusty
conditions, but no precipitation as yet. The instrument
approach in use at Addison was the localizer approach to
Runway 33. ATC cleared the A–36 to descend to 3,000
feet, 800 feet above the initial approach altitude:

> BONANZA THREE–EIGHT–NINER–KILO–
> BRAVO, FLY HEADING THREE–ZERO–ZERO, DE-
> SCEND AND MAINTAIN THREE THOUSAND,
> EXPECT THE LOCALIZER RUNWAY THREE–
> THREE APPROACH AT ADDISON.

The pilot acknowledged the instructions, turned the aircraft, and descended:

> NINER–KILO–BRAVO, ROGER. THREE–ZERO–
> ZERO, OUT OF FOUR THOUSAND FOR THREE,
> EXPECT THE LOCALIZER.

After a few minutes, during which the controller handled several air carrier flights into Love Field and helped
a flight of Air National Guard transports around nearby
cells, the controller handed the Bonanza pilot off to an-

other approach controller for final sequencing on the approach:*

> NOVEMBER THREE–EIGHT–NINER–KILO–
> BRAVO, TURN RIGHT HEADING THREE–TWO–
> ZERO, CONTACT APPROACH ON ONE–TWO–
> FOUR–POINT–THREE.

While banking the Bonanza toward the new heading, the pilot read back the instructions:

> NINER–KILO–BRAVO, ROGER. RIGHT TO
> THREE–TWO–ZERO, ONE–TWO–FOUR–POINT–
> THREE, GOOD DAY.

The pilot listened briefly before switching frequencies to see if the controller questioned the readback. No one said anything, so the pilot retuned the comm radio and checked in with the new approach controller:

> APPROACH, BONANZA THREE–EIGHT–NINER–
> KILO–BRAVO WITH YOU, LEVEL AT THREE
> THOUSAND.

After issuing instructions to several other aircraft, the controller acknowledged the call and issued the final approach clearance:

> NOVEMBER THREE–EIGHT–NINER–KILO–
> BRAVO, REGIONAL APPROACH. DESCEND AND
> MAINTAIN TWO THOUSAND TWO HUNDRED
> UNTIL ESTABLISHED ON THE LOCALIZER,
> CLEARED FOR THE ILS RUNWAY THREE–ONE

---

* A handoff between approach controllers is common practice in crowded airspace, where the TRACON service area is divided among several controllers.

RIGHT. CONTACT THE TOWER NOW, ONE–
TWO–ONE–POINT–ONE.

The terse readback was:

OUT OF THREE FOR TWO–POINT–TWO,
CLEARED FOR THE APPROACH, NINER–KILO–
BRAVO.

Okay, stop here. What just happened? Whose fault is it?
And what, if anything, should the pilot or controller do
about it?

Look carefully at the approach clearance the controller
just issued. The Bonanza is inbound for landing at Addison and was told earlier to expect the Localizer Runway 33
approach. The approach clearance is for the ILS Runway
31 Right. The trouble here is that Addison has no Runway
31, Left or Right. In fact, it only has one runway, 15–33.
So we now know at least part of the problem: The controller issued a clearance for a nonexistent runway.

That's not the whole picture, however. Those familiar
with Love Field in Dallas know that Love (*a*) is only about
8 miles south of Addison, and (*b*) has two main parallel
runways, numbered (you guessed it) 13–31 Left and Right.
Now you can see what's going on: The Bonanza, which
probably appears on the controller's scope somewhere
southeast of both Addison and Love, was cleared for an
approach into the wrong airport.

Understanding what has happened is the first step, but
we still don't know where ATC *thinks* the Bonanza is supposed to go. And until we know where the aircraft is expected to go, we don't know what the pilot should do.
Either:

(a) The controller intended to clear the Bonanza for the
    Localizer 33 approach to Addison, and merely said
    "ILS Runway 31 Right" by mistake.

Or:

(b) The controller misunderstood the Bonanza's desti-
     nation, and intentionally cleared it for the ILS ap-
     proach into Love.

One clue as to what the controller *meant* is found in the
approach clearance. The pilot was told to contact the tower
on 121.1, which is the tower frequency for Addison. But is
this enough information to go on? May the pilot assume
what the controller intended and go ahead with the approach?

Let us analyze the risks of making any assumptions in
this scenario. For starters, suppose Approach expected the
aircraft to go into Love, cleared it to do so, and sequenced
it into the flow of traffic. The local controller at Love tower
is expecting the arrival; the controller at Addison tower is
not. But the pilot assumed the controller *meant* to say "Localizer Runway 33" instead of "ILS Runway 31 Right."
The pilot switches frequencies and calls the Addison tower,
announcing the intention to execute the localizer approach. The Addison tower crew is caught unawares, perhaps expecting other aircraft inbound on the localizer at
the same time. While they scurry around trying to figure
out who in the world this is, the approach controller who
cleared the Bonanza into Love (and the Love Field tower
controllers) sees 389KB's radar target bypass Love Field
altogether and intercept the Runway 33 localizer for Addison. Suddenly, aircraft separation and sequencing at *both*
airports is mixed up, and what was a simple misunderstanding has degenerated into a system-wide communications failure.

At best, the Addison tower will have to contact the TRA-
CON (and Love tower) to figure out where this aircraft is
supposed to be, and must either order the aircraft out of

its traffic area or provide IFR separation for its approach. At worst, the Bonanza could unexpectedly meet up with another aircraft shooting the same approach.

If the situation is reversed, the potential risks are exactly the same. Suppose, this time, that the pilot is familiar with the area, and knows that Love Field has an ILS approach for Runway 31 Right.* If ATC expects the aircraft to land at Addison, but the pilot unquestioningly accepts the clearance for the ILS into Love, then separation at Love may be lost—and, again, confusion will almost certainly result.

If it isn't obvious to you yet, the solution to this example of miscommunication is elementary: The pilot must *ask* the controller for clarification and *must not* make any assumptions. A short transmission will clear up any confusion:

APPROACH, NINER–KILO–BRAVO. DID YOU MEAN TO CLEAR US FOR THE LOCALIZER APPROACH TO ADDISON?

ATC's response will be clear, and no one will be in the dark. The pilot will either hear:

AFFIRMATIVE, NINER–KILO–BRAVO, YOU ARE CLEARED FOR THE LOCALIZER RUNWAY THREE–THREE APPROACH AT ADDISON. CONTACT ADDISON TOWER NOW, ONE–TWO– ONE–POINT–ONE.

Or:

NEGATIVE, NINER–KILO–BRAVO. YOU ARE CLEARED FOR THE ILS RUNWAY THREE–ONE

---

* This is a fair assumption. After all, if the pilot wasn't familiar with Love Field's runway configuration (and didn't know an ILS 31 Right was there), the approach clearance would almost certainly have provoked a question from the cockpit.

RIGHT AT LOVE FIELD. CONTACT THE TOWER
NOW, ONE–ONE–EIGHT–POINT–SEVEN.

Regardless how it comes out, the pilot's simple inquiry
solved any confusion between the parties, and the IFR
system is still functioning. If ATC *thought* the Bonanza was
landing at Love, but the pilot wanted to go to Addison, the
pilot can bring that to the controller's attention and things
can be cleared up that way. In any case, however, the
threat of miscommunication is eliminated, and a harmless
misunderstanding remains just that—harmless.

This situation did, in fact, turn out to be harmless. The
pilot noticed the controller's clearance for the wrong approach and read it back with some skepticism ("Are you
sure . . . ?"). The controller realized the error, issued a
corrected clearance for Addison airport, and thanked the
pilot. The lesson is still there for us to learn, however: But
for the pilot's decision to *verify*, a real problem could have
developed.

How did this happen? Experts tell us that virtually every
aviation mishap, large or small, results from a chain of
events rather than a single, isolated occurrence. In the
"wrong-approach" scenario, you should have picked up on
at least six indicators that a communications gap might be
likely—six cues that alert the wary pilot to listen even more
carefully to ATC and to other aircraft. These factors include: threatened bad weather that breaks concentration
and prompts pilots to rush to get on the ground; numerous pilot requests for deviation, wreaking havoc on
planned traffic flow; a bouncy, low-altitude IFR ride that
can distract a pilot's attention; two airports located near
each other, both conducting IFR operations onto north-
erly runways; a last-minute handoff to a different approach
controller who hadn't discussed "Addison" airport with

the pilot; and a poor, incomplete readback of the final approach clearance by the pilot.

When you notice the presence of any of these factors (or, indeed, of anything that helps set the stage for mixed signals), be more than normally vigilant in all respects, including the attention you give to the radio. It takes little extra effort, and the dividends can be substantial.

Just A Short Count, Please: The Direction Finder (DF) Steer is one of those ATC services that is little-understood and infrequently used. Increased radar coverage, high-tech navigation arsenals aboard even the simplest aircraft, and the decreasing availability of DF equipment have combined to make DF Steers less common than they once were. Nevertheless, DF navigation still comes in handy when a pilot is lost and ATC doesn't have the aircraft identified on radar.

A little background information is appropriate here. A DF Steer is the simplest type of directional guidance a pilot can get without visual reference to known landmarks. It is basically a system whereby the pilot establishes radio contact with one or more ground stations equipped with DF equipment, and the ground personnel "home in" on the pilot's comm radio transmissions. Once the ground station(s) pinpoint the aircraft's position, the pilot is given a heading to fly in order to reach a desired destination.*

In the days when radar coverage was limited and only the military or airlines had transponders, many ATC facilities (control towers, radar facilities, and FSSs) had DF

---

* Usually the pilot asks for vectors to the nearest airport. Any pilot who becomes so lost that a DF Steer is needed is likely to be extremely rattled and in no mood to continue a long cross-country flight.

capability. Today, however, a DF Steer is normally only available from Flight Service—and then only if the aircraft is within DF range. Range becomes more of a problem as Automated Flight Service Stations (or AFSSs) continue to assume the widespread duties of many local FSSs. The remote communications range of each station expands while its DF range does not. Consequently, a DF Steer is not as easy to get these days as it once was. Nevertheless, the DF Steer works as well today as ever, and can be a valuable navigation option for pilots who are lost and are not radar-identified.

Here's how the DF Steer works: Once a pilot establishes voice contact with a DF-equipped ground station, the ground operator instructs the pilot to give a "short count" or "long count." When so instructed, the pilot simply counts aloud on the radio from one to five and back for a short count, or to ten and back for a long count, then stops transmitting. As the pilot counts, the ground operator uses the DF equipment to trace the source of the radio signal and determine the precise compass bearing from the station to the aircraft.

By itself, a single bearing indicates the aircraft's azimuth (direction) from the station, but gives no distance information. The station operator knows only that an aircraft is somewhere along a straight line from the station in a given direction. In order to get a definite fix on the aircraft's location, then, the operator will attempt to get a bearing from another DF station (if the pilot is within range of two different stations) and triangulate the location on the map. If no other stations are close enough, a single DF station can still get an approximate fix by looking at the map along the azimuth line and asking the pilot to look for certain landmarks (if the ground is visible to the pilot). Even if the aircraft's distance from the station remains unknown, the controller can still help the pilot fly a heading directly to that station.

On a warm autumn evening in the late 1960s, one pilot who was lost needed help getting her bearings, but didn't really know how the DF system worked. The result was, quite literally, a complete communications breakdown—and remains a good lesson for IFR communications today.* The pilot, a student, got lost somewhere on the outskirts of Dallas in a single-engine trainer. She was on the third leg of a three-stop flight and, after flying around for an hour or so trying to get her bearings, discovered she was (*a*) really, truly, not-kidding-around lost; and (*b*) getting low on fuel. Fortunately, she was close enough to the Dallas area to call for help. She tuned to the control tower frequency at Love Field (DAL), established contact and explained her predicament. The tower controller told the pilot to stand by, then phoned downstairs to the radar room and asked an approach controller to get a DF fix on the aircraft using the tower frequency.†

When the approach controller was ready, the tower called the pilot and told her they could help her figure out where she was:

CHEROKEE NINER–KILO–BRAVO, I CAN GIVE YOU A DF STEER. GIVE ME A SHORT COUNT, PLEASE.

Controllers in the tower and downstairs in the radar room gathered around to listen to the proceedings.

This pilot appeared not to know what "DF Steer" or "short count" meant. She asked the controller:

* The controllers involved in this sequence of events insist that this account is entirely accurate.

† This was a common practice in the mid- to late-sixties, when few general aviation aircraft were transponder-equipped.

WHAT DID YOU SAY, APPROACH?

The controller's reply was patient at first:

CHEROKEE NINER–KILO–BRAVO, GIVE ME A SHORT COUNT.

Whatever the pilot thought she was hearing, it didn't seem to make any sense. She asked again:

APPROACH, CAN YOU REPEAT THAT?

A few more controllers were gathering around, chuckling at the pilot and at the controller's frustration. The controller called the pilot again, speaking slowly (and sounding more than a little irritated):

CHEROKEE NINER–KILO–BRAVO, I NEED YOU TO GIVE ME A SHORT COUNT.

This apparently still didn't tell the pilot what she needed to know, so she tried once more:

APPROACH, I DON'T UNDERSTAND.

The approach controller had had enough. The other controllers were now smiling or laughing out loud. Exasperated, the controller made it as simple as possible:

NINER–KILO–BRAVO, JUST START COUNTING!

Well, the pilot did just that. She keyed the microphone and began a slow count:

ONE . . . TWO . . . THREE . . . FOUR . . .

The controller engaged his DF equipment and set about fixing the aircraft in space. Engrossed in his indicators, for a few moments he scarcely noticed as the count continued:

TEN . . . ELEVEN . . . TWELVE . . .

Soon the controller had a precise bearing. The pilot was operating somewhere to the northeast of the Love Field area. Several people discussed where she might be located, but the controller wanted her to identify some landmarks. Unfortunately, the count was still underway:

TWENTY-FOUR . . . TWENTY-FIVE . . . TWENTY-SIX . . .

A hush fell over the room; looks of disbelief were exchanged. The controllers stopped laughing as the pilot kept counting:

FORTY-TWO . . . FORTY-THREE . . . FORTY-FOUR . . .

All hell broke loose as controllers scattered. There had been seven other aircraft on the tower frequency, and all were now cut off from the controllers by what amounted to a stuck microphone.

FIFTY-NINE . . . SIXTY . . . SIXTY-ONE . . .

Grabbing for their landline telephones, controllers alerted other ATC facilities in the area that the approach frequency had changed due to a "problem" on the frequency in use at the time.

SEVENTY-SEVEN . . . SEVENTY-EIGHT . . .

Eventually, all the aircraft on the tower frequency gave up and either called Love Ground Control or Approach Control and received an alternate frequency for the Love tower.

Controllers recounting this incident say the pilot counted to almost one hundred without a break. As a result, all normal operations on the tower frequency were frozen for almost two minutes (an eternity on a busy frequency). A complete communications loss, no matter how brief, can be terrifying to pilots and controllers alike. Fortunately, the only harm that resulted was a few racing pulses and some rewritten clearances. The pilot was given vectors back to her destination airport. She landed without incident, albeit without much fuel to spare.

While it's obvious what the pilot did wrong, it's also obvious why she did what she did. She did exactly what she was told, but carried it to the extreme. If she had stopped to think about it, she would have known she was tying up the frequency and, after several minutes, wasn't any closer to finding out where she was.

The controller shares the blame equally, both for losing his composure and for failing to explain what he wanted. It was clear that the pilot had no idea what a DF Steer or a short count was; the controller could have spelled it out for her.

The lesson from this example is both obvious and subtle. The obvious part is that you should ask for an explanation any time you don't understand something, and you should use common sense when it comes to tying up a busy frequency. The subtle message is this: At times throughout your flying career, you will hear instructions, phrases, names, fixes, procedures, clearances, or requests on the radio that you've never heard before and/or don't understand. When this happens, the safest course is to play dumb, and ask the speaker to explain. Even if you *think* you know what someone else means, never act on that belief unless you are *sure*.

Pay Attention, Dammit: It is axiomatic that being an effective communicator means *listening*. Being attentive is part of your job as pilot-in-command. Nearly every occurrence of actual radio confusion includes at least a hint of inattention by one party to what the other is saying. A dramatic example of such a lapse occurred northwest of San Antonio International Airport.

Approach Control was busy with the morning rush hour. One inbound arrival was AirCarrier Flight 853, an MD-80 operated by a foreign national airline. The flight was about 110 miles out and level at 10,000 feet, waiting for a lower altitude. The weather was severely clear, with 25 miles of visibility. Winds were light and variable, with simultaneous visual approaches to Runways 12 Left and Right in use.

To keep the flow of traffic going smoothly, the TRACON was directing traffic around to the north and west of the city, then issuing vectors for straight-in visual approaches. Aircraft approaching San Antonio from the east and south would descend over town from the lower flight levels to 10,000 feet, then turn around for a southeasterly arrival.

Approach would offer inbound traffic a choice of the left or right runways, clear each flight for the visual approach to that runway, then hand the aircraft off to the local controller:

AEROSTAR THREE–BRAVO–MIKE, REPORT THE AIRPORT IN SIGHT. CAN YOU ACCEPT RUNWAY ONE–TWO LEFT?

The Aerostar pilot replied that the airport was in sight and Runway 12 Left would be just fine. The controller issued the approach clearance:

NOVEMBER ONE–THREE–BRAVO–MIKE IS CLEARED FOR THE VISUAL APPROACH RUNWAY ONE–TWO LEFT, CONTACT THE TOWER ONE–ONE–NINER–POINT–EIGHT.

The same pattern was repeated over and over on the approach frequency. If they had been paying attention,

AirCarrier 853's pilots would have heard the controller ask flight after flight about runway preference, then clear each for the visual approach to "One–Two" Left or Right.

When it was AirCarrier 853's turn to be sequenced in for arrival, Approach called to ask the crew's runway preference:

AIRCARRIER EIGHT–FIFTY–THREE, REPORT THE AIRPORT IN SIGHT. CAN YOU ACCEPT RUNWAY ONE–TWO RIGHT?

The frequency was fairly busy at the moment, so the fact that Flight 853 didn't answer right away wasn't surprising. What happened next, however, was. The controller checked in with a couple of other arrivals, waited a few more seconds, and called Flight 853 again:

AIRCARRIER EIGHT–FIFTY–THREE, SAN ANTONIO APPROACH. REPORT THE AIRPORT IN SIGHT, CAN YOU ACCEPT RUNWAY ONE–TWO RIGHT?

The pilot's reply, in heavily accented English, sent chills down the controller's spine:

EIGHT–FIFTY–THREE, ROGER. LEVEL AT ONE–TWO.

A glance at the MD-80's data block on the radar scope confirmed the controller's fears. Sure enough, the pilot of 853 had *climbed* from 10,000 to 12,000 (or "One–Two Thousand"). Somehow, the crew had misunderstood the radio call and construed a question about "One–Two" to be a climb clearance.

The real threat in this situation was the presence of other aircraft descending to 10,000 feet in the opposite direction of the airliner. The MD-80 had climbed right up into the flow of approaching traffic. By instructing Flight 853 to descend *immediately* to 8,000 feet, giving a few quick "level-off" commands to descending aircraft, and issuing several vectors, the approach controller was able to resolve three threatened traffic alerts, with no loss of separation. Flight 853 landed without incident.

This is a case in which you can pinpoint one primary factor that contributed to the mixup: inattention by the flight crew of AirCarrier 853. It's surprising, to say the least, that a professional crew of two Airline Transport Pilots could sit level at 10,000 feet, listening as Approach handled numerous aircraft ahead of them, yet be caught completely off guard by a simple question. Furthermore, it is inconceivable that an airliner would accept an instruction to *climb* during the arrival phase of a flight without asking questions.

Even if the controller had inadvertently told 853 to "climb and maintain One–Two Thousand," the pilots had a duty to verify such an instruction when common sense suggested it was a mistake. More likely, what happened was that the pilots, for some reason or other, didn't hear *all* of the controller's call. That, in itself, is no great sin. If the crew had been running decent checklists, verifying approach speeds, etc., they might have been talking and missed part of the first call. What was really inexcusable was the crew's failure to ask Approach to "say again." Even if they *thought* they heard a command to climb to 12,000 feet, the pilots still should have read back the command:

AIRCARRIER EIGHT–FIFTY–THREE, ROGER. LEAVING ONE–ZERO THOUSAND FOR ONE– TWO THOUSAND.

A readback like that would certainly have caught the controller's attention and averted the problem entirely.

When you factor in such items as the frequency congestion during the rush hour and the pilots' use of English strictly as a second language, it's possible to sympathize (a little bit) with the pilots. Still, the fault for this scenario lies completely with the flight crew. Aviation is something man may harness, but can never completely control. Beautiful and fascinating, it is always dangerous; it is most unforgiving of even the briefest lapse of attention. In a Piper Cub, such a lapse could damage an aircraft or even cost the pilot's life. In an airliner, inattention can kill hundreds.

Nonverbal Radio Communication: Most people are familiar with nonverbal communication, the ability to transfer ideas or information to another without using the spoken or written word. For an aircraft in IFR flight, one piece of equipment allows the pilot to communicate nonverbally with ATC: the transponder. The transponder normally serves as a means for ATC's radar to distinguish your radar return from those of other aircraft in your area. It is also used to tell controllers (without words) that you are VFR, that you have lost radio communications, that you have an emergency aboard, that your aircraft is being hijacked, or perhaps that yours is a military operation.

Initially, when an aircraft is detected on radar without a corresponding transponder return, it is shown only as a "primary" return, a simple blip on the screen indicating that something is out there. If that aircraft is equipped with an operating transponder, however, the primary return will soon be "tagged up" by ATC's computers. Transponders are sensitive to ATC radar. When a radar sweep is detected, your transponder is "interrogated," and it replies to the interrogation by transmitting your squawk code back to the radar receiver.*

"Tagging up" describes what occurs during takeoff when your aircraft first climbs high enough to register on ATC radar. The ATC computer recognizes your squawk code and calls up your flight information from its records. The computer then labels, or "tags" your aircraft's radar return on ATC's radar screens with a data block containing your tail number, aircraft type, altitude, ground speed, or other information.

The data block that identifies your aircraft on radar is important to ATC, because the controllers along your route are expecting you. They have your route information in front of them, they know what other aircraft are in the area, and they need to know without question which aircraft is which.

As mentioned in chapter 13, your IFR flight plan is automatically opened when your flight tags up on radar. It's easy to imagine the kind of havoc that results within the ATC system if one aircraft takes off using the wrong transponder code. Squawking an incorrect code can cause a variety of problems. Sometimes, if the code you're using incorrectly isn't assigned to anyone else, the error has little effect. At worst, it's like taking off with the transponder turned off or set to "standby"—the computer won't tag up your return, and your aircraft remains unidentified. In that case, as soon as a tower or departure controller notices this "nonidentification," you'll be reminded to verify that you are squawking the proper code.

Other times, however, such a mistake can cause more

* Before departure, your transponder should be preset to the squawk code you received in your clearance. Unless ATC advises differently, you will continue to squawk that code throughout your flight.

trouble. If you preset a squawk code that is supposed to be used by *another* aircraft, and that other aircraft hasn't yet tagged up on radar, the computer will tag your radar return with the other flight's statistics. This is *mis*identification, a more serious problem than nonidentification. Your call sign, route, requested altitude, aircraft type, and everything else will be wrong. It you take off in a G–IV and turn west at 250 knots climbing at 4,000 feet per minute, you might just startle a controller who—based on the tag on your radar return—thinks you're northbound in a Stearman.

Unfortunately, the problems caused by squawking the wrong code go farther than misidentification. By taking off with someone else's code in the window, you open that aircraft's IFR flight plan. Even if you (or ATC) discover and correct the error immediately after you tag up on radar, the other aircraft's flight plan must be flushed and re-entered into FAA's system. If that other aircraft was ready to depart (or is already rolling), ATC may find itself handling one or more aircraft in IFR conditions without a flight plan. Confusion is always hazardous in IFR operations, but it is most threatening when ATC is confused as to *who* you are (or *where* you are).

The phenomenon of aircraft tagging up with the wrong code is more than just pilot error in copying a clearance or presetting the transponder. It's usually the result of someone transposing two or more digits (e.g., 6023 becomes 6203). You may think this sort of error is random in nature and is likely to result in mere nonidentification most of the time; but unfortunately, the computer-assigned squawk codes within a given area are usually similar for similar flights. For example, three aircraft scheduled to depart from the same airport at around the same time might be assigned codes 4035, 4045, and 4055.* As a result, one wrong digit here or there often means an aircraft isn't just unidentified, it's actually usurping another's squawk code.

The misidentification of two aircraft departing Logan International nearly resulted in a traffic conflict (and certainly caused confusion among controllers) in the Boston TRACON area. The two were airliners, both departing north on Runways 4 Left and Right. They picked up their clearances, containing similar squawk codes, within minutes of each other on 121.65, Logan's clearance delivery frequency. AirCarrier Flight 355 Heavy, bound for Miami, picked up its clearance and its assigned squawk code of 2755. AirCarrier Flight 276 was cleared to Kansas City and told to squawk 2765. It's not clear where the actual errors occurred, although a review of ATC tapes established that the clearance delivery controller read the proper codes to each aircraft and received a correct readback from each.

Flight 276 taxied to Runway 4 Left; 355 Heavy was sent to the departure end of 4 Right. The initial departure instructions—included in their clearances—were as follows:

(a) Flight 276 (on the left runway) was cleared to turn left heading 030° for vectors to join Victor 308, climb and maintain 5,000 feet.

(b) Flight 355 Heavy (on the right) was to turn right to

---

* Although it's not readily apparent, there seems to be a method to ATC's madness in assigning squawk codes. Most IFR pilots have had the experience of filing both legs of a round-trip flight at the same time, and upon completing the first flight and copying the return clearance, discovered that the squawk code for the return is nothing more than a variation of the code for the first leg (e.g., you were assigned 3244 for the trip out and 3422 for the return).

050° for vectors to PVD (Providence), climb to 9,000 feet.

So here you have two aircraft preparing to depart from parallel runways, turn slightly away from each other, and climb through the same altitudes until one levels at 5,000 feet. This isn't an uncommon situation; many large airports use parallel departure runways and have aircraft turn slightly apart after takeoff.

The only trouble here was (you're starting to get the picture, right?) that the two flight crews reversed their transponder code assignments: the 355 Heavy crew had preset 2765 on their transponder, and the crew of 276 had 2755 on theirs. "Okay," you think, "so they've got each other's codes. That's not a big problem, because each will activate the other's flight plan, and they can simply swap back to the correct codes when ATC notices the mistake." Well, that's partly true. If two aircraft depart at the same time and tag up with each other's flight plan, they can simply reset their respective transponders and everything will be fine. Remember, however, that the two flights are supposed to turn left and/or right on departure. This factor changes things significantly.

Both aircraft were cleared for takeoff—first 276, then 355 Heavy—within thirty seconds of each other. The local controller was aware of the relative positions of the two aircraft and knew their paths were to diverge as soon as they departed their runways. As both aircraft passed over the boundary, two overlapping targets appeared on the radar display in the tower cab. The controller noted that the targets corresponded to the positions of the two aircraft, and instructed both to contact Departure Control.

The Boston departure controller noted the data tags for

both flights, and watched for the two to separate. Like the tower controller, the departure controller also knew that 276 would be turning left and 355 Heavy would turn right. The radar display depicted the two aircraft as one large return, with their data blocks set apart from each other for better readability. Unfortunately, they were tagged in reverse: The one on the left was labeled AC 355H, and the other appeared to be AC 276. As each aircraft reached a safe altitude, they banked away from each other. As Flight 276 headed to the left, however, the controller's display indicated that *355 Heavy* was turning left—directly into the flight path of what appeared to be Flight 276. Before the controller could react, 276's heading changed. It was turning *right*—bringing it closer still to 355 Heavy.

The controller issued immediate instructions to both aircraft:

AIRCARRIER THREE–FIFTY–FIVE HEAVY,
TURN RIGHT IMMEDIATELY, HEADING ZERO–
FIVE–ZERO, BREAK; AIRCARRIER TWO–
SEVENTY–SIX, TURN LEFT IMMEDIATELY
HEADING ZERO–THREE–ZERO.

Puzzled acknowledgments came back from both pilots, who were confused not only by a command to do something they were already doing, but also by the controller's use of "immediately," a term reserved only for very urgent instructions. Flight 355 Heavy's first officer spoke up first:

AH, DEPARTURE, THREE–FIFTY–FIVE HEAVY
IS ALREADY FLYING ZERO–FIVE–ZERO, OUT
OF FOUR THOUSAND TWO HUNDRED FOR
NINER THOUSAND.

The captain of Flight 276 then chimed in:

DEPARTURE CONTROL, TWO–SEVENTY–SIX IS
LEVEL AT FIVE THOUSAND, WE'RE FLYING
ZERO–THREE–ZERO AT THIS TIME.

During the few seconds it took for these exchanges, the
controller watched as the primary targets for each aircraft
separated safely from each other. After the targets themselves split, the corresponding data blocks crossed over
one another and followed the targets in different directions. Instantly, the controller knew what had happened:
These two flights had been misidentified. After checking
the flight progress strip for each, the controller asked both
crews to verify what they were squawking. The swapped
numbers were identified, and both aircraft recycled their
transponders to the proper codes. One or two radar
sweeps later, the data blocks for the two targets had reversed themselves. Traffic separation was maintained and
the controller was able to breathe again.

This particular event was fairly benign, both in origin
and effect. Yet, as with most examples of miscommunication, confusion resulted, and the delicate fabric of the ATC
system was strained for a few moments. The lesson it provides is summed up by the comments of one of the controllers involved in this incident:

Like I always tell pilots, I'm used to watching you to
see if you do what your clearance says. I see people bust
altitudes or turn the wrong way all the time. That's why
minimum separation still keeps aircraft miles apart. But
when you tag up with the wrong identifier, I don't know
who you are or where you are. If I don't know that, I
can't watch out for you. I can't vector you. I can't even
see you. If you only get *one thing* right in your entire
clearance, get the squawk code right. So long as I know

which radar target is which, we can work out the rest.

In the previous example, both aircraft read back the proper squawk code to clearance delivery. Yet both managed, somehow, to dial in the wrong code. It's an easy enough mistake to make; you handle enough numbers during an IFR flight to fill a phone book. But it's also a simple error to avoid with just a few extra steps. During clearance copying, pay close attention to the squawk code (it's normally the last item in the clearance). When you read it back, do so slowly. *Immediately* after reading back the clearance, dial the code into the transponder and set the unit to "standby" (or "off," if you haven't started the engines yet). Add *"transponder check"* to your runup checklist. Verify that the unit is warmed up and set to the proper code. Finally, when you are ready for takeoff, switch the unit on (and to Mode C or S if so equipped).

In a radar environment, your transponder is the only thing that distinguishes you from every other aircraft in the area. Be sure yours identifies you properly.

Did I Really Hear That? One of the pitfalls of radio communications is overanticipation of what ATC will tell you to do. At first glance, this statement might appear at odds with the teachings of this book—that you should anticipate each situation in an IFR flight and know what to say beforehand—but it's possible to carry things too far. While it's true you should endeavor to "stay ahead" of IFR communications the same way you stay ahead of the aircraft, you can overdo it to the point where you stop listening to what ATC actually says. Those who are so used to being given the same clearances, altitudes, and frequencies on the same routes are the ones most likely to hear what they *expect* to hear and miss out on important details.

Commuter airline pilots who operate out of smaller fields are especially susceptible to overanticipation. They fly the same routes up to five or six times a day, into and out of airports where theirs are about the only scheduled flights. The clearances begin to sound like broken records, containing the same route, altitudes, frequencies, and (sometimes) even the same squawk codes. It can get to the point where the pilot knows what the clearance will say before the clearance delivery controller does.

Santa Fe County Municipal Airport in Santa Fe, New Mexico, is one such airport where commuters make up the only scheduled traffic on a daily basis. For the crews of a King Air C–90A and a Metroliner commuter flight, the complacency that comes with repetitive operations led to some excitement in the clouds over the mountains of northern New Mexico. A commonly used route for commuter traffic from Santa Fe into the Albuquerque, New Mexico, area is direct to FLYBY intersection, then into ABQ via the Friho Two Arrival.

CommuteAir Flight 2990, a Metroliner, filed for a 2245 Zulu departure from Santa Fe to Albuquerque. They had requested the standard route into ABQ, with a cruising altitude of 18,000 feet. The captain called for the clearance, although she could almost certainly have copied it in her sleep. Having flown the same route twice already that day (and nearly a hundred times in the last few months), she knew what the route and altitudes would be: Cleared as filed, maintain 8,000 feet, expect 14,000 after ten minutes.

The weather was warm and gusty, with the ATIS reporting broken layers at 1,500, 4,000 and 7,000 feet (a.g.l.). As expected, the Metro was cleared via the standard route:

COMMUTEAIR TWENTY–NINE–NINETY IS CLEARED TO ALBUQUERQUE INTERNA-TIONAL AIRPORT AS FILED. MAINTAIN EIGHT THOUSAND, EXPECT ONE–FOUR THOUSAND AFTER TEN MINUTES. DEPARTURE FRE-QUENCY ONE–THREE–TWO–POINT–EIGHT, SQUAWK FOUR–NINER–FIVE–SIX.

The captain copied the clearance, and the ground con-troller reported that the readback was correct.

As the Metroliner climbed out from Runway 2, the first officer was flying the airplane. The captain checked in with Departure Control, expecting to be cleared (as usual) all the way up to 14,000 (the altitude they'd been told to "expect" after ten minutes):

ALBUQUERQUE CENTER, GOOD AFTERNOON, COMMUTEAIR TWENTY–NINE–NINETY WITH YOU, OUT OF SEVEN–POINT–FOUR FOR EIGHT THOUSAND.

Unknown to the commuter's crew, however, there was inbound traffic overflying the area: a King Air heading northwest at 14,000 feet. The controller responded with a vector and a climb clearance.:

COMMUTEAIR TWENTY–NINE–NINETY, ALBU-QUERQUE CENTER, GOOD AFTERNOON. RA-DAR CONTACT, TURN LEFT HEADING TWO–FOUR–ZERO, CLIMB AND MAINTAIN *ONE–TWO* THOUSAND.

At this point in the flight, the crew of the Metroliner was busy establishing climb power, cleaning up the aircraft, and running through the climb checklist. The captain ac-knowledged the vector and clearance:

LEFT TO TWO–FOUR–ZERO, OUT OF EIGHT
FOR *ONE–FOUR,* COMMUTEAIR TWENTY–
NINE–NINETY.

The departure controller didn't reply to flight 2990's
readback, even though the altitude was wrong. It would be
several minutes before anyone would notice.

Climbing through 12,000 feet, the Metroliner entered a
bumpy layer of broken cumulus clouds. By the time the
flight leveled at 14,000, the ride was smoother but the
aircraft was in solid IFR conditions. The afternoon sun on
the nose of the airplane brightly illuminated the cloud
interiors. Both pilots squinted in the white glare, occasionally catching a glimpse of blue sky above.

The flight crew was startled from its reverie by a strange
call from the departure controller:

COMMUTEAIR TWENTY–NINE–NINETY, TURN
RIGHT IMMEDIATELY THIRTY DEGREES, SAY
ALTITUDE.

The crew, alarmed and puzzled by the transmission,
rolled the Metro into a tight bank and replied:

COMMUTEAIR TWENTY–NINE–NINETY IS
LEVEL AT *ONE-FOUR* THOUSAND.

In describing the incident later, the captain of Flight
2990 stated she wasn't sure what happened next, but re-
called hearing an instruction to descend immediately to
12,000 feet just as a shadow appeared in the windshield,
obscuring the glare of the clouds for an instant. Both pilots
blanched as their minds processed the image their eyes
had recorded: A large twin had just appeared in the cloud
from the left, passing just off the left wingtip and

across the nose. It looked like a King Air, and it had been close enough so that 2990's crew could read the tail numbers *even though both aircraft were still in the clouds.*

The pilot of the other airplane, operating at an assigned altitude of 14,000 feet in clouds, never saw the Metroliner. If the King Air's flight path had taken it just a few more feet to the right, neither flight crew would have seen what hit them.

Unless a controller speaks up and challenges a readback, most pilots will (correctly) assume they read an instruction back accurately. In the situation described above, it's possible that the pilot's use of abbreviated language (e.g., "Out of Eight for One–Four" instead of "out of Eight thousand for One–four thousand") contributed to the controller's failure to notice when the captain said they were leaving 8,000 feet for 14,000. It's also possible that the controller was thinking ahead to another operation for another aircraft. Whatever the reason, however, no one noticed the Metro's excursion above 12,000 feet until it was almost too late.

The stage for this kind of error is set anytime a pilot sets out on an all-too-familiar route. Just as you can get lost when operating over unfamiliar terrain, you can get lulled into a false sense of security when flying the same routes and clearances day after day. This phenomenon is not unique to copying altitude clearances, of course. There seems to be a kind of "proficiency middle ground" among pilots, a maximum level of safety that they achieve in a particular operation. For most, this high point comes as a combination of training and experience. After you finished your instrument training, chances are you were physically adept at controlling the aircraft, sharp on partial-panel work, and well-versed in the FARs. You lacked experience in hard IFR, however, and so only possessed part of what you require to be a skilled IFR pilot. Others who have been flying IFR for years have the finesse and confidence that comes with experience, but may have lost that "knife edge" attentiveness and responsiveness of the newly trained student. The finest instrument pilots, then, are those in the "middle ground"—those who are both sharp on the controls *and* wide awake with excitement. They have enough experience to be more precise, but are not so comfortable as to be asleep at the stick.*

What happened over New Mexico undoubtedly changed the lives of the pilots involved. The lesson they learned is this: You can never, ever assume you will receive a specific route, frequency, squawk code, or altitude. Copy every clearance as though it were the first time you'd flown the route, and *always* write down a new altitude assignment before climbing or descending. Keep asking yourself, "Did I really hear what I think I heard?" If your answer is anything other than an unqualified yes, you'd better call ATC back and find out the whole story.

I Thought You Called Them: Earlier chapters dealt with the procedure for canceling your IFR flight plan with ATC. One way or another, you've got to be sure the flight plan is closed at the end of the flight. If you land at a tower-controlled airport—no problem. The flight plan is closed as soon as you land. However, when the tower is closed (or if the field is uncontrolled), you must either cancel IFR before landing or notify ATC after you arrive. When you

---

* In order to keep themselves aware of the dangers of overconfidence (and to stay sharp on emergency procedures), most experienced pilots insist on some sort of regular proficiency training. Insurance companies and risk managers observe that, statistically, the pilots in the "middle ground" of experience are far safer than those very high-time pilots who don't participate in proficiency programs.

execute an approach, land, and shut down the aircraft, ATC loses contact with you. If you don't somehow contact the authorities and wind up the flight plan, controllers have no way of knowing where you are or what has become of your aircraft.

Anytime ATC loses radio and/or radar contact with an aircraft on an active IFR flight plan, machinery is set in motion to locate the flight. If the pilot left a telephone number on the flight plan, ATC tries to contact the pilot or someone who knows about the status of the flight. Controllers phone different airports or other facilities, inquiring into the plane's whereabouts. If ATC gets no satisfactory explanation for the loss of contact, it will initiate search-and-rescue efforts.

Most pilots are aware of their responsibility to close a flight plan when landing at those airports with no control tower. If they know they're landing at the East Treetrunk airstrip, they are prepared to notify ATC by phone after arriving. They plan the flight that way, and usually they remember to call soon after landing. Conversely, those who file flight plans into tower-controlled airports rarely consider the need to notify ATC of anything after the flight. They know the flight plan is closed when they land, and that's all there is to know about it.

This notion, unfortunately, is only correct if the destination airport is served by an operating tower *around the clock*. What about those airports (comprising the vast majority of tower-controlled fields) where the tower is closed overnight? If you're planning a flight into an airport where the tower closes at sunset, or at 10:00 P.M. local time, or at midnight, or on holidays, you'd better think about what time you'll be arriving in the area. If there is a chance the tower will be closed when you get there, you should prepare yourself to: (*a*) make traffic advisory broadcasts on the CTAF; (*b*) shoot the approach without a tower clearance to land; and (*c*) contact ATC after landing to close your flight plan.

On a clear September evening, the crew of a Lear 31 were returning from Washington National to their home base at Pal-Waukee Airport (PWK), northwest of Chicago. The flight had been uneventful, and the approach controller with the Chicago TRACON was only moderately busy as the Lear approached from the east, over Lake Michigan. O'Hare traffic was landing to the northwest, and the Naval Air Station at Glenview was quiet, so the controller brought the Lear in near Glenview and set it up for a visual approach to Runway 34 at PWK.

The Lear's original ETA into PWK was to have been 8:30 P.M. local time. Outbound traffic delays at DCA, however, had kept the aircraft on the ground for an extra forty minutes. As the jet was crossing the shore of Lake Michigan, south of Glenview, the approach controller issued the following instructions:

LEARJET THREE–EIGHT–NINER–KILO–BRAVO, DESCEND AND MAINTAIN THREE THOUSAND. ADVISE PAL-WAUKEE IN SIGHT.

The flight crew had spotted the beacon at PWK before crossing the shoreline:

APPROACH, NINER–KILO–BRAVO HAS THE AIRPORT IN SIGHT. OUT OF FOUR THOUSAND FOR THREE.

The controller watched the jet's Mode C return indicate a rapid descent to 3,000 feet, then vectored the aircraft into the PWK traffic area:

NOVEMBER THREE–EIGHT–NINER–KILO–
BRAVO, TURN RIGHT HEADING THREE–ZERO–
ZERO, CLEARED FOR THE VISUAL APPROACH
RUNWAY THREE–FOUR AT PAL-WAUKEE. CON-
TACT THE TOWER NOW, ONE–TWO–FOUR–
POINT–SEVEN.

This was a common approach clearance for the flight
crew, and the first officer repeated it from memory:

RIGHT TO THREE–ZERO–ZERO, CLEARED THE
VISUAL THREE–FOUR, AND ONE–TWO–FOUR–
POINT–SEVEN; NINER–KILO–BRAVO. GOOD
NIGHT.

At this point, both controller and pilot had made a simple mistake—they hadn't looked at the time. It was 9:10
P.M.; the Pal-Waukee tower had closed at 9:00 P.M. From
closing time until 6:00 A.M., PWK becomes an uncontrolled
field with a CTAF (119.9 MHz). When the tower controllers shut down, they switch the ATIS to an "overnight"
announcement. The Learjet crew, unfortunately, had listened to the ATIS about twenty minutes earlier, while the
airfield was still open, and so hadn't heard the overnight
tape.

The first officer switched to the tower frequency and
tried to check in:

PAL-WAUKEE TOWER, LEARJET THREE–
EIGHT–NINER–KILO–BRAVO IS WITH YOU AT
THREE THOUSAND, ON THE VISUAL AP-
PROACH FOR THREE–FOUR.

Needless to say, no one responded on 124.7. After several more attempts, both the captain and first officer realized it was after hours. They switched to the CTAF, heard

other traffic in the area, and announced their presence. As they flew the approach, the crew continued proper CTAF calls until they landed and were clear of the active runway.

After the approach and landing, the crew shut down, secured the aircraft, and went home. All was fine until 2:30 A.M., when the captain was awakened by a phone call. It was the company's chief pilot, calling at the behest of the FAA to locate the crew of a Lear 31 that had disappeared while on an approach into PWK. It turned out that the aircraft's IFR flight plan was never closed with ATC, and a frantic search of the flight plan records led the FAA to the chief pilot. Fortunately, full-scale search-and-rescue efforts hadn't been initiated, since there had been no reports of a downed aircraft anywhere in the heavily populated Chicago area. The captain later said he assumed the approach controller had canceled IFR for the flight; the first officer said that they hadn't discussed it. The captain should have known, however, that a controller may only cancel an IFR flight plan if the pilot requests it. There is no "automatic" cancellation unless the tower is open and informs the TRACON that the aircraft has landed.

The FAA didn't take any action against either pilot for failing to close a flight plan, although they might have tried. Arguably, the controller was equally at fault for failing to tell the crew to "change to advisory frequency approved" instead of to "contact the tower." But assigning fault isn't the point. Even though this example doesn't include any near-misses or lost aircraft, it points out that when you discover a mistake of some kind, you must think through *all* of the possible consequences and respond to them. The crew should have done two things when they discovered the tower was closed: Switch to the CTAF (which they did), and realize they would have to close their IFR flight plan after landing (which they did not do).

What would you have done in this situation? What if Approach hands you off to a tower that turns out to be closed? If the weather is clear and you are on a visual approach, switch back to the approach frequency and re-establish contact with ATC. Tell them that the tower is closed and you'd like to cancel IFR with them. You will earn a gold star in the heart of the controller and you won't have to worry about calling anyone after landing. If you need to execute the entire approach, do so while making regular announcements on the CTAF. After you land and are ready to shut down, call Approach on the radio (if you can reach them) and cancel IFR. If you can't make radio contact from the ground, phone the nearest FSS or ATC facility and close your flight plan with a specialist. Either way is equally effective, although the telephone route invariably takes longer. The important thing, however, is to somehow close the flight plan; you will spare others needless inquiry and may save yourself a great deal of embarrassment.

Your Brother's Keeper: This next episode not only illustrates a common mistake, but highlights the need for you to listen to what *everyone* is saying on the radio, even if they aren't talking to you. Occasionally, you may detect a communications error that doesn't involve you directly. If such a mistake goes unnoticed by those involved, you should intervene if the opportunity presents itself. Pilots, arguably, have a moral obligation to assist others in safe operations when they can. This means listening to the entire radio "picture" in your area and getting a feel for who is operating nearby and who is being cleared to go where. If you hear a controller issue a vector or clearance and the readback is incorrect (or comes from the wrong aircraft), *speak up.* If you don't want to identify yourself, don't—but at least transmit something that will alert the affected parties to a potential problem.

In this case, a Cessna Skyhawk called Atlanta Approach and asked for a VFR clearance to transit the Atlanta TCA and land at Dekalb-Peachtree, a satellite airport on the far side of the TCA. Other aircraft in the area heard the following exchange:

ATLANTA APPROACH, CESSNA THREE–EIGHT–NINER–KILO–BRAVO IS JUST SOUTH OF PALMETTO, VFR AT FOUR THOUSAND, NORTHBOUND FOR LANDING AT DEKALB-PEACHTREE.

The controller responded with a squawk code and altimeter setting:

NOVEMBER THREE–EIGHT–NINER–KILO–BRAVO, ATLANTA APPROACH, ROGER. SQUAWK TWO–SIX–SIX–ONE AND IDENT, HARTSFIELD ALTIMETER THREE–ZERO–ONE–ONE.

The pilot read back the squawk code and the controller went on to communicate with other aircraft for a few moments. Later the controller acknowledged receiving the Cessna's transponder return:

CESSNA THREE–EIGHT–NINER–KILO–BRAVO RADAR CONTACT, ONE–SIX MILES SOUTHWEST OF THE ATLANTA VOR. FLY HEADING ZERO–TWO–ZERO, MAINTAIN TWO THOUSAND.

The pilot replies:

NINER–KILO–BRAVO, ROGER. ZERO–TWO–ZERO, MAINTAIN TWO THOUSAND.

After hearing this conversation, alarm bells should be going off in your mind. What's wrong? And what should you do about it?

The error occurred in the altitude assignment. In his initial radio call, the pilot of 389KB told the controller the aircraft was level at 4,000 feet. The controller later instructed the aircraft to "maintain two thousand." The problem is, the aircraft wasn't cleared to *descend and maintain* 2,000. The controller has made one of several possible errors:

(a) She meant to say "maintain *four* thousand" instead of "maintain two thousand."

(b) She meant to say "*descend* and maintain two thousand."

Or:

(c) She thought the Cessna was already level at 2,000 feet, and wanted it to stay there.

Whatever the controller meant, the instruction was simply "maintain two thousand." The pilot reacted merely by reading back the altitude, and so is also guilty of one of several mistakes:

(a) He thought the controller said "maintain four thousand," so stayed level at that altitude.

(b) He heard the controller say "two thousand," but *assumed* she meant 4,000—and so stayed level anyway.

Or:

(c) He heard the controller say "maintain two thousand," but assumed this clears him to *descend* from 4,000 to 2,000 feet. As a result, he reduces power and begins the descent to 2,000.

All this happened within a few seconds on a busy approach frequency. You overheard the exchange, and you believe the pilot and the controller misunderstand each other. Besides asking yourself what this error could mean to the people involved, you should also consider whether—and how—you will react. Should you assume that the controller will eventually clear the aircraft to 2,000 feet anyway, eliminating any risk? Do you figure the aircraft is staying at 4,000? Will you do anything at all? Do you even notice?

Before you answer, consider the risks posed by this simple mixup. If the controller *meant* to keep the aircraft at 4,000 feet and it descends to 2,000, there may be a loss of separation for other aircraft operating at that altitude. Likewise, if the controller meant for the Cessna to be level at 2,000 feet and the pilot stays level at 4,000, conflict may result at that altitude. But perhaps the least obvious risk is conflict during the *descent itself*. While it is unlikely that the controller has a bunch of 737s cruising around level at 2,000 feet, the Cessna may be descending through 3,500–2,500 feet just as it crosses the approach/departure corridor for turbojet traffic from Atlanta Hartsfield's parallel runways. If other aircraft are climbing or descending through the 3,500–2,500-foot block near the Cessna, the potential for separation loss increases drastically.

A review of the actual outcome in this case revealed the following: The controller knew the Cessna was level at 4,000 and wanted it level at 2,000. She should have said "descend and maintain two thousand," but accidentally omitted the words "descend and." After being told to *maintain* 2,000 the Cessna assumed this was a descent clearance and descended to the new altitude. Cessna 389KB was safely vectored to Dekalb-Peachtree and landed without incident.

In this situation, then, both sides erred but nothing came

of it. To some extent, errors like this occur hundreds of times a day and are never noticed because nothing happens to call the FAA's attention to them. Nevertheless, as you can see, there was a brief "communications failure," and the safety margin for aircraft in the area could easily have been compromised.

So what would you do if you heard this situation develop while you were operating in the area? If you hear evidence that the two sides of a conversation are going in opposite directions and you notice that neither side is aware of the misunderstanding, try a simple radio call to one side or the other:

APPROACH, DID YOU MEAN FOR CESSNA
NINER–KILO–BRAVO TO *DESCEND* AND MAIN-
TAIN TWO THOUSAND?

Notice that this transmission doesn't even mention your call sign. Nevertheless, such a call in the blind will likely stimulate either Approach or 389KB to call the other and verify the other's intentions, and that should head off any threatened conflict.

The same principle applies no matter what the mistake is and no matter who made it. When the wrong aircraft acknowledges an instruction and no one else notices, tell the controller. If ATC issues a descent clearance and the pilot reads back the wrong altitude, call it to the pilot's attention if the controller doesn't. You have nothing to lose and everything to gain by helping others avoid trouble.

Quick Lessons

An alert, conscientious pilot learns something about flying during every flight. Each time you fly, whether it's for two-tenths of an hour or two days straight, ask yourself a few questions when the flight is over: What things did I do wrong? What things went wrong that I could have or should have taken care of? What did I do on this flight that I would do differently, given the chance? Introspection like this is a healthy, humbling practice. Be constructively critical of yourself. You'll learn something new about flying with every hour you log, and you'll be a little safer each time you go up.

This section comprises a few quick lessons, as related by several different pilots, learned during otherwise "routine" flights. Not only will you find the lessons themselves instructive, you should also get a feel for the kinds of things to watch for—and learn from—as you become a better IFR communicator.

I Said "Right": An instrument flight instructor and a student in a Skyhawk took off on Runway 18 of a small, controlled airport for an instrument-training flight. They were to fly to a practice area some 30 miles to the east of the airport. The pilot secured a VFR clearance through the nearby ARSA and was cleared for takeoff. The takeoff clearance, however, was unusual:

NOVEMBER THREE–EIGHT–NINER–KILO–
BRAVO, AFTER TAKEOFF TURN RIGHT HEAD-
ING ZERO–NINER–ZERO, RUNWAY ONE–EIGHT
CLEARED FOR TAKEOFF.

Note that the clearance was for a *right* turn from Runway 18 to a 090° heading—a 270° turn. The pilot either didn't notice the unusual instruction or assumed the controller meant to say "turn to heading Zero–Niner–Zero" instead of "turn right."

The Cessna lifted off and flew over the runway until reaching a safe altitude. The pilot began a turn to heading

090°, but it was a *left* turn. The flight instructor immediately wrenched the yoke in the other direction, banking into a standard-rate turn to the right. The student was puzzled, but the instructor offered no explanation other than "wait." As the plane rolled out onto the new heading, ninety seconds later, the student's eyes widened. A Boeing 727, northbound on final approach to the nearby hub airport, descended across the Skyhawk's flight path from right to left, approximately 2 miles away. The student quickly realized where a left turn to 090° would have put the airplane—one to two miles closer to the airliner, if not directly in its path.

The lesson is obvious: If a controller issues you a new heading and tells you to turn the "wrong" way, *ask* about it. Never, never assume you know what a controller means. Unless you're told otherwise, "right" means right; "left" means left. It's not enough, after all, to get to the right airport if you fly the wrong route. Likewise, it's not enough to arrive at the correct heading if you get there the wrong way—or at the wrong time.

What's in a Name? Most air traffic controllers know the three-letter identifiers for navaids, fixes, and airports in their respective service areas. Occasionally, however, they come across identifiers they don't recognize. If you and the controller on the other end of the frequency use different names or identifiers, you could end up seriously misplacing yourself or the airport.

The two most common causes of name-versus-identifier mistakes are (*a*) the use of similar identifiers for navaids within a fairly small area, and (*b*) the use of unofficial names for navaids by pilots or controllers.

Similar names: In north Texas, for example, the Acton VORTAC (identifier AQN) is just southwest of Fort

Worth, while the Waco VORTAC (identifier ACT) is only 50 miles to the south along Victor 17. If you were a controller and had to read clearances with both "ACT" and "Acton" in them, what would you do? You'd run the risk of mixing them up, that's what. What if you were a pilot copying a clearance with "direct Acton" in it? You might write down "ACT." One controller from Fort Worth Center estimated that at least eight or ten aircraft per day get "ACT" and "Acton" mixed up.

Unofficial names: In many parts of the country, navaids or airports have "nicknames" that are known well to controllers and pilots who operate in the area, but are foreign to those from out of town. One such location is the Hoosier VORTAC (identifier OOM), located at Bloomington, Indiana. Roughly 130 nautical miles away is Bloomington, Illinois, home of the Bloomington VOR (identifier BMI). Until recently, OOM was designated BMG and was *also* named "Bloomington." It seems there was too much confusion (oh, really?) over which Bloomington was which, and the FAA decided in 1988 to redesignate the Indiana VORTAC as Hoosier/OOM. No problem.

There is a fly in the ointment, however. Controllers and pilots alike throughout the Midwest still refer to OOM as "Bloomington." In *IFR* magazine, writer Jeff Parnau told of one flight in which three different controllers—a clearance delivery controller in Wisconsin, a departure controller at Milwaukee, and an en route controller at Chicago Center—all referred to OOM as "Bloomington" on the air. Either old habits die hard or people are resorting to *locations* (and not official names) for navaids.

The risk inherent in this practice is staggering. There are navaids and airports named "Marion" in Illinois, Indiana, and Ohio, not to mention four "Marion County"

airports scattered about the southern states. If you mention "Fulton" or "Fulton County" to another pilot, be sure
to mention whether you're talking about the airport in
Ohio, Georgia, Indiana, Missouri, or New York. You can
fly to Sky Harbor Airport in Phoenix, Arizona, or you can
find airports with the same name in Illinois, Nevada, and
Minnesota. Nevertheless, each of these locations has a
unique three-letter identifier, the purpose of which is to
avoid confusion about navaid and airport names.

The solution to misread (or miscopied) clearances is to
ask a controller to use full phonetic identifiers when reading your clearance, whether it's the initial clearance or
something simple like "proceed direct XYZ when able."
Most controllers won't mind such a request. Some, in fact,
may prefer to read the identifier rather than try to remember all of the names. When read with identifiers, a clearance between the Waco and Acton VORTACs reads
"Alpha–Charlie–Tango, Victor One–Seven, Alpha–
Quebec–November." A flight across the Hoosier VOR-
TAC takes you via "Oscar–Oscar–Mike." A clearance limit
to "Foxtrot–Tango–Yankee" ends up at Fulton County in
suburban Atlanta, instead of "Foxtrot–Tango–Tango,"
Fulton Municipal Airport in Missouri.

Insist that controllers use identifiers anytime you're in
unfamiliar territory. They are a bit more cumbersome to
say, but they are also much simpler, and more accurate, to
copy.

What Was That Vector Again?   You already know that you
should read back every vector and altitude clearance in
case you and the controller are thinking along different
lines. Most of us were taught that when issued a vector, we
are to go ahead and begin the turn as soon as we hear the
instruction, and read it back when we can during the turn.

This is ordinarily a sound practice. Starting your turn right away means reaching the new heading sooner, and controllers really appreciate quick compliance with instructions. Sometimes, however, you've got to stop, think, and verify a vector before you execute the turn. If you receive a heading or other instruction at what seems like a strange time, or if the vector will take you somewhere you'd rather not go (e.g., across the departure end of an active runway), call back and verify the instruction before you turn.

One pilot who stopped to question a vector literally saved the day as well as her instrument rating. The pilot had been operating along Florida's west coast near St. Petersburg, doing airwork, partial panel, and holds. She was taking the check ride for the instrument rating and so had one passenger—an FAA examiner—in the right seat of the Piper Archer. After two successful approaches into Whitted, a neighboring airport, the Archer was cleared north toward St. Petersburg/Clearwater International (PIE) for landing. Tampa Approach handed the Archer off to the St. Petersburg tower, and the tower instructed the pilot to enter a right downwind for Runway 17 Right. The aircraft was on a heading of 360°, south and slightly east of PIE. In order to enter the right downwind, the pilot turned left twenty degrees to 340° and proceeded toward the airport at 2,000 feet.

Seconds after she leveled the wings, the pilot heard an anxious controller's voice:

CHEROKEE NINER–KILO–BRAVO, TURN IMMEDIATELY HEADING THREE–THREE–ZERO, A NAVAJO OFF ONE–SEVEN LEFT CLIMBING THROUGH ONE THOUSAND FIVE HUNDRED.

When a controller says "immediately," that means *right now*. But the pilot hesitated—that new vector didn't make sense. How would a ten-degree turn to the left make any difference if there was a traffic problem? The pilot reached for the push-to-talk button to verify the instruction.

In the seconds it took for the pilot to question the new heading, the flight examiner in the right seat pointed to a growing shape just to the left of the nose. The pilot rolled hard right and dove, and the departing Navajo screamed past at what was later judged to be roughly a quarter of a mile—just about 1,500 feet.

The pilot and examiner reported the near-miss. Several discussions with ATC later, it was determined that the controller had meant to order a "right turn to Zero–Three–Zero" instead of "turn to heading Three–Three–Zero." If the Archer pilot had complied with the first instruction, the ten-degree left turn might well have resulted in a collision. By trusting her instincts, and questioning an instruction that somehow just didn't seem right, the pilot caught and corrected a nearly fatal mistake. She also got her instrument rating that day.

Go Ahead: The instruction "Go ahead" is official, approved phraseology for pilots and controllers. You'll find it in the Pilot/Controller Glossary of the *AIM* (see chapter 3). It's also one of the most oft-misunderstood terms in ATC's lexicon, even when it's used correctly.

"Go ahead" is what a controller or pilot says when it's okay to *go ahead with your radio transmission.* It is *not* used to grant permission to *do* anything (except speak). When you call Center and say, "Niner–Kilo–Bravo has a request," and the controller responds, "Niner–Kilo–Bravo, go ahead," this means "I'm listening; what can I do for you?" But if you call and say "Niner–Kilo–Bravo, request permission to deviate left around a cell," you should *never* hear "Go ahead" in response. That term is only used when someone else is ready to listen to you talk. If ATC okays your request to go around the storm cell, the controller will say, "Niner–Kilo–Bravo, deviation approved," or something to that effect.

Controllers rarely misuse "go ahead." On those occasions when you ask for a clearance to do something in particular, and all the controller says is "Niner–Kilo–Bravo, go ahead," that's because ATC didn't hear or understand your entire request. On a crowded frequency, if your request is interrupted by another aircraft, you'll hear "Other aircraft requesting deviation, go ahead." Again, this means "Talk to me," not "Do what you want."

One of the most common settings in which people misunderstand "go ahead" is during ground operations. At a busy airport, a ground controller may handle five aircraft on the ramp for every one operating in the local controller's airspace. Ground control frequencies can get congested, and the controller may not hear every word of a request.

Suppose a pilot rolls out on landing and is told to contact Ground when clear of the runway. The pilot turns off and calls, "Treetrunk Ground, Bellanca Three–Eight–Niner–Kilo–Bravo is clear of One–Seven Right at Hotel, taxi to terminal." The ground controller, busy pulling up a clearance, heard the aircraft call but didn't catch the entire request. A glance at the runway tells the controller that the Bellanca has stopped on taxiway Hotel, so he proceeds to issue an IFR clearance to another aircraft that had called a minute earlier.

After the clearance is issued and read back, the Bellanca pilot, still waiting patiently off 17 Right at Hotel, calls again. "Treetrunk Ground, Bellanca Three–Eight–Niner–Kilo–Bravo." The controller calls back, "Bellanca Niner–Kilo–Bravo, go ahead." Well, that's all the authorization the pilot needs; so the brakes are released, the throttle goes forward, and the Bellanca lurches across 17 Left just as a light twin is on short final. The result: One go-around, two angry controllers, and a flustered pilot who can't understand what all the fuss is about.

The pilot should have stayed put until the controller said, "Taxi as requested," "Taxi to parking," "Hold short of One–Seven Left," or some equally specific instruction. You, likewise, should always insist on a clear, unequivocal clearance for any operation (ground or otherwise). If you are *ever* told to "go ahead," even if it's used in a sentence ("Go ahead and cross the runway"), insist that the controller rephrase the instruction. Ask if you are *cleared* to cross runway XX, if you are *cleared* to taxi to parking, or whatever. Don't run the risk of "going ahead" into trouble.

Oh, You Meant a Full Approach: Next time you have a book of approach plates in your hand, flip through and notice how many of them contain the notation "NoPT" somewhere in the plan view diagram. The abbreviation means No Procedure Turn Required, and usually applies to aircraft being vectored for an approach or aircraft that arrive at the final approach fix more or less lined up for the approach. In areas of low-altitude radar coverage, procedure turns are rare, except for training flights. A full procedure turn roughly doubles the duration of an approach, and that means more work for controllers and higher fuel costs to pilots.

When you are "cleared for the approach," you have permission to execute an instrument approach procedure to the airport (and runway) mentioned in the clearance. Most pilots assume, therefore, that it's okay to fly the *full* approach, as shown on the chart (procedure turn included), unless specifically told otherwise by ATC. Many note that

NoPT means that a procedure turn is not *required;* therefore, the logical inference is that the turn is not *prohibited,* either. This was once true, but not anymore. The FAA has added the following notation to the explanation of NoPT as found in the NOS approach charts: "Procedure Turn shall not be executed without ATC clearance."

Almost every approach controller has stories of pilots who, after being vectored for a non-precision approach in a busy area, decide to fly the procedure turn without telling anyone. The inevitable result is the scattering of aircraft to the right and left of the approach course while this "rebel without a clue" flies out, around, and back to where he was in the first place.

Next time you're expecting an approach that contains a procedure turn, you can take two steps to avoid any confusion: (1) Listen; and (2) Ask. *Listen* to the approach controller as other aircraft are cleared into the airport. Is a non-precision approach in use? Are planes being vectored onto the final approach course, or are they cleared first to the NDB over the airfield (thus making a procedure turn mandatory)? Next, when it's your turn to be cleared for an approach, *ask* ATC if you should proceed inbound or fly the complete approach. Avoiding an unnecessary procedure turn will save you time and fuel—and maybe a lot more.

CHAPTER 18

Parting Shots

As I stated at the outset, this book is not offered as the be-all and end-all of communications handbooks. It doesn't tell you, "This is what to say to the controller at this moment." Rather, it's intended to give you a better understanding of *who* all those people you talk to during IFR flight are, *why* you have to talk to them, and *what* they want to know. Once you get the different phases of instrument flight in your mind and you think about what controllers want from you, that I-don't-know-what-to-say feeling goes away and is replaced by a quiet confidence when you use the radio.

Being an effective IFR communicator requires a little forethought, a little common sense, a little practice, and almost no talent. On nearly every IFR flight you will hear some poor pilot somewhere stumble through poorly phrased radio calls that more or less completely fail to tell the controller what the pilot wants to do. As the airwaves become increasingly congested, we have less room for this pilot on the radio or in the system.

You, as a working component of the IFR system, must not allow ambiguous, incomplete, or inaccurate communications to affect your flight; they have no place in your daily operations. You wouldn't tolerate inattention or inaccuracy in any aspect of your IFR flying, whether in aircraft maintenance, training, flight planning, preflight inspection, stick-and-rudder technique, navigation, or flying approaches. It makes little sense, then, to accept anything less from yourself as an IFR communicator.

When you're suspended inside a cloud miles above the earth, the radio is your only bond to the Air Traffic Control system and a safe passage home. It is my sincere hope that this book has served to reinforce that bond.

Appendix

The ICAO Phonetic Alphabet

Character	Code	Name	Pronunciation
A	·−	Alfa	Al-fah
B	−···	Bravo	Brah-voh
C	−·−·	Charlie	Char-lee (or Shar-lee)
D	−··	Delta	Del-tah
E	·	Echo	Eck-oh
F	··−·	Foxtrot	Focks-trot
G	−−·	Golf	Golf
H	····	Hotel	Hoh-tell
I	··	India	In-dee-ah
J	·−−−	Juliett	Jew-lee-ett
K	−·−	Kilo	Kee-loh
L	·−··	Lima	Lee-mah
M	−−	Mike	Mike
N	−·	November	No-vem-ber
O	−−−	Oscar	Oss-kah
P	·−−·	Papa	Pah-pah
Q	−−·−	Quebec	Keh-beck
R	·−·	Romeo	Row-mee-oh
S	···	Sierra	See-air-ah
T	−	Tango	Tang-go
U	··−	Uniform	You-nee-form

V	· · · –	Victor	Vick-tah
W	· – –	Whiskey	Wiss-kee
X	– · · –	X-Ray	Ecks-ray
Y	– · – –	Yankee	Yang-kee
Z	– – · ·	Zulu	Zoo-loo
0	– – – –	Zero	Zee-row
1	· – – – –	One	Wun
2	· · – – –	Two	Too
3	· · · – –	Three	Tree
4	· · · · –	Four	Fow-er
5	· · · · ·	Five	Fife
6	– · · · ·	Six	Six
7	– – · · ·	Seven	Sev-en
8	– – – · ·	Eight	Ait
9	– – – – ·	Niner	Nyn-er

Index

263